D0125400

More Advance Praise for Scott D. Anthony's *Little Black Book of Innovation*

"*The Little Back Book of Innovation* distills two decades of research and real-world experience into the ultimate reference guide for novices and veterans of the Innovation Wars. **A vital handbook for leaders seeking to teach and evangelize the power of innovation.**"

—Colin Watts,
Chief Innovation Officer, Walgreens

"*The Little Black Book of Innovation* is rich and insightful with actionable tips to increase your organization's innovation capacity. It's easy, engaging, and **essential reading for business leaders and their teams that will ignite innovative thinking in your organization.**"

—Melanie Healey,
Group President North America and Global
Hyper-Super-Mass-Channel, Procter & Gamble

"At Ayala, we know we have to become more innovative to compete in quickly changing markets. That's why we've worked closely with Scott Anthony and his team to develop our leaders' innovation skills. *The Little Black Book of Innovation* brings together the best of Anthony's experiences and insights into **an easy-to-understand, supremely practical book.**"

—Jaime Augusto Zobel de Ayala,
Chairman and CEO, Ayala Corporation

Praise for Scott D. Anthony's
The Silver Lining

"A valuable playbook for bringing disruptive innovation into the enterprise at a time when many corporations are pulling back on their innovation initiatives."

— Dominic Basulto, Big Think

"The lessons that Anthony draws from times of great economic upheaval are useful any time and anywhere."

—Rolf Dobelli, getAbsract.com

"In tough times, companies often hunker down and focus on the core. But those companies that stop innovation are sowing the seeds of their own destruction. *The Silver Lining*'s practical tools can help companies innovate successfully."

—Vijay Govindarajan, professor, Tuck School of Business at Dartmouth College; Professor in Residence and Chief Innovation Consultant at General Electric

"*The Silver Lining* clearly shows that companies can successfully innovate in the face of change. Put this book's ideas to work today."

—Michael Mauboussin, Chief Investment Strategist, Legg Mason Capital Management

"Anthony's playbook is a welcome source of hope for those of us in the midst of the Great Disruption. Required reading for companies experiencing cataclysmic change."

— Mark Contreras, Senior Vice President/ Newspapers, the E.W. Scripps Company

THE
LITTLE
BLACK BOOK
OF
INNOVATION

Also by Scott D. Anthony

Seeing What's Next: Using the Theories of Innovation to Predict Industry Changes, with Clayton M. Christensen and Erik A. Roth

The Innovator's Guide to Growth: Putting Disruptive Innovation to Work, with Mark W. Johnson, Joseph V. Sinfield, and Elizabeth J. Altman

The Silver Lining: An Innovation Playbook for Uncertain Times

THE
LITTLE
BLACK BOOK
OF
INNOVATION

‖ HOW IT WORKS ‖
‖ HOW TO DO IT ‖

SCOTT D. ANTHONY

HARVARD BUSINESS REVIEW PRESS
BOSTON, MASSACHUSETTS

Library of Congress Cataloging-in-Publication Data

Anthony, Scott D.
    The little black book of innovation: how it works, how to do it/
Scott D. Anthony.
        p. cm.
    Includes bibliographical references.
    ISBN 978-1-4221-7172-1 (alk. paper)
    1. Technological innovations—Management.   2. Business planning.
3. Technological innovations—Management   4. New products.
5. Success in business.   I. Title.
    HD45.A678 2012
    658.4'063—dc23

                                                        2011025139

To Joanne, as always.

CONTENTS

PREFACE

In the middle of 2010, I ran an experiment. I told the subjects of the experiment—my colleagues at Innosight, a professional-services firm that specializes in innovation—that my goal was to learn which innovation books they would recommend to colleagues. I asked them about ten books that I probably heretically called Innosight's canon—five authored by Innosight's cofounder Clayton Christensen, two authored by Innosight board member Richard Foster, and three authored by members of Innosight's leadership team. For each book, survey takers could note that they had read the whole book, read most of the book, skimmed the book, or not read the book at all.

The three books that interested me the most were those that I assumed would be most pertinent to our staff—*The Innovator's Solution* (the work that lays the theoretical grounding for most of Innosight's work), *The Innovator's Guide to Growth* (a step-by-step playbook that explains how we do our work), and *Seizing the White Space* (at the time Innosight's latest work). Only *half* of the consultants—people who spend every day advising clients on issues of innovation and growth—reported reading most or all of these three books (clients, don't fret—we have an apprenticeship model and excellent training programs to make sure our consultants deliver stellar service). This is not an uncommon result. One publisher told me her figures showed that 90 percent of business books that customers purchase are never read.

And that's why I wrote this book. Innovation increasingly affects all of us. Decades of research and field work point the way to innovation success. My aim is to take this work and make it more accessible by sharing simple anecdotes that I've collected over the last decade. I hope this "black book" of innovation serves as an everyday reference that helps you make the changes that will allow you to succeed in your business or personal lives. I've seen how following the approaches here have helped big companies, entrepreneurs, and my friends and family members, and I hope what follows will help you, too.

MY INNOVATION JOURNEY

My personal innovation journey forms the foundation of *The Little Black Book of Innovation*. That journey began in earnest on an airplane on Friday, October 20, 2000. I don't have a photographic memory, nor do I keep a detailed diary, but this particular moment coincided with an event that can be dated—Pearl Jam's October 21, 2000, concert at Desert Sky Pavilion in Phoenix.[1]

In my carry-on bag was a book—*The Innovator's Dilemma* by Harvard Business School professor Clayton Christensen. I was a second-year student at HBS and was in

---

1. I did have to do a little research to confirm that the concert was in fact on a Saturday. Thanks, setlist.fm! From this Web site, I learned that my concert was one of ten times that Pearl Jam has played "Timeless Melody" by The La's, live. The wonderful uselessness of the Internet certainly makes writing books more pleasurable. And greetings to footnote readers. You'll note the footnotes here are not academic references—they are parenthetical or personal comments. Unless otherwise presented in the footnote, the full bibliographic details of any source discussed in this book are given in the appendix and endnotes.

an experimental course Christensen was teaching for the first time: Building a Sustainably Successful Enterprise.[2]

The first day of class was interesting. Christensen ambled into the room, hunching his shoulders to get his six-foot-eight-inch frame through the door. Despite his imposing physical presence, Christensen spoke softly. He described how his primary passion this time of year was Duke basketball, because his oldest son—who is an inch taller than Christensen—was a center on Duke's team.[3] Christensen then did something that felt amazingly anachronistic at HBS in 2000—he lectured for a good sixty minutes about his research and core beliefs using acetates on an overhead projector. It was a stark break from most HBS courses, which were typically interactive and case-based. Some people got turned off. I leaned forward in my seat, listening attentively to Christensen's compelling message.

On that Friday flight to Phoenix, I read *The Innovator's Dilemma*. It's a bit cliché to say that flight changed my life, but hey, clichés exist for a reason. I got more and more passionate about Christensen's research, and his ideas. I did

2. In my year, there were two 80-student sections of what became known as BSSE, both taught by Christensen. In the 2009–2010 academic year, there were seven 100-student sections, with a four-person team of Christensen and three well-regarded former executives teaching the course. In other words, more than 75 percent of the 880 students who constituted the HBS Class of 2010 took BSSE. I was what the innovation literature would call an early adopter.

3. That team went on to win the 2000–2001 NCAA Championship, with Christensen's son Matt averaging 8.4 minutes, 2.6 points, and 1.3 rebounds a game during the regular season. Matt would later work with us at Innosight for a few years before going to HBS himself and forming a company called Rose Park Advisors to do equity investing based on his father's research.

independent research for Christensen during my last semester at Harvard, took a job heading up his research activities after graduation, wrote a book with him, and, in 2003, joined Innosight, the professional services company he had cofounded in 2000.

I found Christensen's research exhilarating. I had held a perception, surely shared by many readers, that innovation and growth were just random. Here was someone who drew on a diverse range of case studies and academic research to counter that viewpoint. Christensen showed how there were actually patterns that dictated success and failure. The implication was that by studying and applying the patterns, people could improve their ability to succeed with innovation. I would quickly learn that Christensen was one of a small group of scholars and practitioners joined in a quest to make innovation a predictable discipline (chapter 2 describes select members of this group).

The notion of bringing predictability to innovation immediately resonated with me, but to be honest, I wasn't exactly sure why. Then I finally put my finger on it. I had needed this disciplined understanding of innovation when I faced my own innovator's dilemma back in 1995.

My Early Innovation Experiences

I've been focusing exclusively on innovation for more than a decade now. In that time, I've been a researcher, a writer, a strategic adviser to large and small companies, an entrepreneur building businesses in the United States and in Asia, and an investor in start-up companies. My innovation experience actually predates these experiences; innovation has in fact surrounded me my entire life. I came to learn that my grandfather, who we'll meet in more depth in chapter 1, introduced a powerful business model innovation in the 1960s. In the late 1980s, my mother launched a business called RelayNet, which was a precursor to the Internet. In an alternative universe, she ended up becoming America Online founder Steve Case, selling RelayNet to Time Warner for billions (unfortunately, in this universe, she transferred ownership to another bulletin board owner for nothing). My mother also pitched a book idea in the early 1990s for a series of books that provided simple, step-by-step instructions for how to use computers under the title *Up and Running*. The publishers thought the idea wouldn't sell. Tens of millions of For Dummies copies later . . . Fortunately for my family's psychological balance, my mother found a place where she could devote her energy and passion—breeding a line of champion Labradors.

As I was growing up, my family was always an early adopter of new technologies. I remember playing *Star*

The author in 1995, taking a break from work at *The Dartmouth*.

Raiders on our Atari 2600, *MicroLeague Baseball* on our Commodore 64, *One on One: Larry Bird vs. Dr. J* on our Apple II, and *Tecmo Bowl* on our Nintendo.[4] I was active on RelayNet in my teenage years, even writing an application that one poor soul paid $25 to register.[5]

Fast-forward to my college years, the setting for my innovator's dilemma. By day I was an economics major, and I took my studies seriously. By night I was active in *The Dartmouth*, Dartmouth College's five-day-a-week paper. I was an accidental journalist. Honestly, I joined the newspaper because the one commitment I made to myself upon coming to Dartmouth was that I would find a serious extracurricular activity. Although I was happy that I had gotten into Dartmouth, getting rejected as an undergraduate by Harvard and Stanford stung.[6] And it was pretty obvious to me why I was rejected, as my most serious out-of-school activity in

---

4. Time for a bit of Anthony family lore. The Nintendo was the first purchase that I made with money I actually earned (aside from allowance money). My source of income? Mowing lawns. My first lawn gig (at age twelve) occurred thanks to the wonders of an alphabetical school directory. Someone called up and asked if I mowed lawns. I asked my parents if I mowed lawns. They said sure. They provided the capital equipment (the mower); I got to keep the proceeds. A few weeks later, Mario was all mine!

5. The application was what was known at the time as a "BBS door." It let people participate in NFL pools, competing to see who could correctly pick the outcomes of each week's game. If I recall correctly, the free version was completely random; the subscription version allowed you to enter in the real schedule. I can't recall if I actually cashed that sole registration check.

6. I went 0-for-3 at Stanford—not making the cut at its business school or at an executive education program (it claimed it didn't allow consultants). I now have a theory that the business schools at Harvard and Stanford implicitly collude to keep their yields (the percentage of admitted students who accept admittance) high by having Harvard take all the students with even social security numbers. I also am skeptical that the moon landing happened. Seriously.

high school was serving as a founding member of the Young John Madden's Fan Club.[7]

I wandered into the newspaper's offices in Robinson Hall in the fall of 1992 and almost immediately fell in love. A few years later, when I went to work in management consulting, I would learn that journalism is a lot like consulting. You have a problem that you have to solve in a pretty short time. You gather as much data as you can, synthesize that data, and present it back in an easy-to-understand format. I began spending almost all of my free time at the newspaper, eventually rising to managing director, in charge of the editorial side of the newspaper.

It turned out that my time at school coincided with the beginnings of a technological revolution. On August 9, 1995, Netscape went public, an event that essentially marked the beginning of the Internet economy. Dartmouth was a particularly wired campus—even then, every student was required to have a computer, and almost all campus communication ran through a simple, ubiquitous e-mail program called BlitzMail. Since I was a bit of tinkerer (I had taken a Web site design class for kicks and designed a site to track my fantasy baseball team), the newspaper's president (my longtime friend Justin Steinman) asked me to come up with a strategy for our Internet operations.

---

7. That's not a joke, sadly. For those who are not fans of American football, Madden was the coach of the Oakland Raiders in the 1970s and a well-regarded television announcer from 1979 to 2008. He also licensed his name to a popular line of Electronic Arts videogames.

I cringe when I look back at the 1995 article that explains the strategy that I cooked up. The article starts by describing why we ended up being one of the last Ivy League newspapers to go on the Internet. The quote stares out at me: "We have a relatively small staff and it wasn't high on our list of priorities." Justin had the article's last word, noting that we'd update the Web site weekly because, "*The D* makes a significant amount of revenue from subscriptions."

What did Justin mean? Too-frequent updating might threaten the core of our business model. In fact, about two-thirds of our $250,000 in annual revenue came from subscriptions. When we first saw the Internet, our first feeling was fear. We were scared of what would happen if we put our content up for free, and we had no idea how we'd charge for it. That fear led to us moving slowly.

We got over that fear, of course. After all, we were college kids who didn't have to worry about meeting analyst expectations or defending ten-year plans to our board of directors. So what did we decide to do? Did we look at this as an opportunity to break free of the shackles that confined us to the bucolic isolation of Hanover, New Hampshire? Did we say, "Cool, a chance to reinvent ourselves and try to do something different"? Unfortunately, no.

"There will be people going through the Web," I said in 1995, "who will see the page and say, 'Gee, I'd like to subscribe to *The D*.'"

Instead of trying to do something cool and different, we tried to force-fit the new technology into our old way of doing business. My team at *The Dartmouth* and I had a chance to use the Internet to rethink our business, and we completely blew it. The opportunity was there. And we missed it.

The Cost of Constrained Innovation

Over the last decade, I have come to realize that we were members of a big club—call it the Innovation Wannabes. The club includes people who had the opportunity to successfully innovate, to create exciting new offerings and business models that turn into vibrant, profitable enterprises, and who failed. My mother is a member of the club. Christensen's research shows how executives from onetime great companies like Digital Equipment Corporation; Sears, Roebuck and Co.; Sony; Blockbuster; and General Motors are in the club. Individuals who have struggled to make the changes that they knew were necessary in their personal lives are in the club.

We all wish we were in another club—call it the Innovation Maestros. A select few, whether by luck or by skill, seem to have mastered innovation. The iconic innovator of our age is surely Steve Jobs from Apple. I have never met Jobs, so I can't say I have any unusual insight into him. But he is constantly portrayed as a creative genius who just sees things that other people can't see and then, through sheer force of will, marshals resources to realize his vision. If the only hope for would-be innovators is to possess Jobsian genius, we're doomed. We will never get past the velvet rope that guards this club.

This rope acts as a significant drag on the world economy. Entrepreneurs feel they have to give a huge chunk of their companies to venture capitalists to have any hope of succeeding. Companies spend literally billions of dollars to advertise products that customers don't really want. Desperate growth-seeking companies will make Hail Mary acquisitions when the research clearly shows that large acquisitions, on average, destroy value.

Large companies are capable of—and often do—amazing things. But these firms just scratch the surface. The talent of their people, the technologies in their labs, and their global capabilities are constrained, held back by a mix of fear and misunderstanding. Too many would-be beautiful businesses that could reinvent markets and create substantial value live only in PowerPoint documents, never to be launched. And of course, there is huge psychic cost to individuals who want to change—who know they need to change—but just can't.

Road map to *The Little Black Book of Innovation*

You don't have to be Steve Jobs to succeed at innovation. My past decade of working with companies, entrepreneurs, and government leaders has led to a strong personal conviction that there is tremendous innovation energy within every individual and every company. A precious few realize their full potential. But innovation is within the grasp of many more.

The good news is, to borrow a phrase from the popular 1990s television show *The X-Files*, the truth is out there. It is in the writings of the academic researchers who have decoded many of the mysteries of innovation. It is in the learning from forward-thinking practitioners who have picked up this academic work and brought it to the field, figuring out what happens in the laboratory that constitutes today's business world.

Much of this learning is out of reach of the layperson. It is locked up in books that are too dense, or even worse, it is locked up in the heads of individuals. *The Little Black Book of Innovation* aims to address this issue by providing the tools and giving you the confidence to more reliably turn your dreams into reality.

I've organized this book into two main parts. Part 1 provides the book's foundation. Chapter 1 describes the innovation imperative—what innovation is, and why *all* of us need to and *can* get better at innovation. Chapter 2 introduces twelve masters of innovation, whose tools should be in anyone's black book. Chapters 3 and 4 draw on these tools to detail four mindsets that empower innovation and seven pitfalls to avoid.

Part 2 introduces a twenty-eight-day innovation program. Each day in the program provides practical tools you can use to answer some of the most common questions facing the would-be innovator. The program is broken into four weeks:

- Week 1: Discovering Opportunities

- Week 2: Blueprinting Ideas

- Week 3: Assessing and Testing Ideas

- Week 4: Moving Forward

Of course, you don't have to do the program in the specific order that I suggest—each day's tip is meant to be largely self-contained. The book's conclusion includes a table that summarizes the program.

This book is not comprehensive, nor does it attempt to provide a unifying innovation framework. Its goal is to give you enough to get started, to make innovation seem more approachable, and to provide pointers to where you can go to learn more.

You'll get the most out of the material that follows if you have already identified an opportunity for innovation. It could be a project you just started at work. It could be a problem that has been nagging you for years. The problem could be big or small; it could be something at home or at the office. Pick something where you could use some inspiration. As chapter 1 argues, the need to get better at innovation is *the* imperative in today's quickly changing world.

PART ONE

LAYING THE FOUNDATION

CHAPTER 1

THE INNOVATION IMPERATIVE

Innovation—something different that has impact—is
both more important and more accessible than ever
before.

Innovation. The very word exudes optimism. Innovation gives us new ways to communicate with friends and family. It helps us live happier, healthier lives. But what does the word mean, and how much does it really matter? This chapter provides a simple definition of innovation, describes different types of innovation, explains why innovation is the most pressing challenge of our time, and details why innovation is more accessible than many realize.

Innovation Defined

Over the past few years, I have written several books on innovation, totaling close to a quarter million words. I went back and looked, and in not one of those books do I actually define what innovation is. That's a glaring oversight. After all, you can't implore readers to be better at something without telling them what that something is.

For a word that is thrown around so much, innovation lacks a clear and consistent definition. In August 2010, a popular innovation blog posted an article listing twenty-five separate definitions.[1] The author was certainly trying to be helpful by producing the list. But how would twenty-five often contradictory definitions help anyone actually do anything with innovation?

The *New Oxford American Dictionary* describes *innovate* as "make changes in something established, especially by introducing new methods." That's not a bad starting point. But I go with something even shorter: "Something different that has impact." Five words. That is the definition of innovation I will use for the rest of this book.

Hidden in that simple statement are a few nuances. For example, it is important to clarify "different" *according to whom*. Innovation is in the eye of the beholder. The innovation *target*—whether it be an end customer, a supervisor, a spouse, or a friend—should be the one who considers it different. And what does impact mean? In my language, impact means some kind of measurable result—whether it

---

1. To be fair, the article at blogginginnovation.com was a collection of suggestions from readers. But the definitions sure ran the gamut. You had something as simple as "Value + Creativity + Execution" and something as complicated as "Creativity is what happens when imagination has focus; innovation is what happens when creativity has a bottom line; enterprise is what happens when innovation meets ability, entrepreneurship is what happens when all the aforementioned are put on the same cart and passion becomes the fuel." I do recommend reading this blog, by the way.

be profit, improved performance of a process, a measurable effect on someone's life, or something else entirely.

Note a few things that are *not* in my definition. The word *technology* doesn't appear; innovation comes in many flavors (I'll discuss this more later). Note the absence of the word *creative* or the phrase *never been done before*. It is always important to separate creativity and invention from innovation. There is a popular conception that innovation is all about a creative idea. Creativity is a piece of the innovation puzzle, for sure. And creativity, of course, can help the innovation process. But innovation is a process that combines discovering an opportunity, blueprinting an idea to seize that opportunity, and implementing that idea to achieve results. Remember—no impact, no innovation.

One way to visualize the difference between innovation and creativity is to compare Leonardo da Vinci and Thomas Alva Edison.[2] Both men were geniuses. If you read through da Vinci's notebooks, you can't help but be blown away by his ability to see the future. He had sketches of devices that look a lot like modern helicopters. He mapped out the human body in remarkable detail. He was a creative genius. Did his ideas meet our definition of innovation? No, because those ideas didn't have impact in da Vinci's time. And that's important to remember, because when we set out to

---

2. This example came out of 2007 work we did with Linkage, a leading executive training company based in Burlington, Massachusetts. We were trying to simplify our materials so that Linkage-trained instructors could teach it to wider audiences inside companies. One of the members of the Linkage team developed this comparison.

innovate, we should make sure we don't fall into the trap of turning it into an academic exercise where we think, think, think, but never do. The doing is the thing.

Edison *did*. He is the consummate innovator. The stock ticker-tape symbol, phonograph, incandescent light bulb, and modern motion-picture industry all had their roots in Edison's labs in New Jersey. They all were different. They all had impact. And that, my friends, is an innovator.

Three Innovation Stories

Let me introduce my grandfather: Robert N. Anthony Sr. My grandfather was inducted into the Accounting Hall of Fame in 1986. Such a place exists! The Ohio State University created it in 1950. As of 2010, it had more than eighty members.[3]

The primary reason my grandfather (who passed away in 2006) resides in the Accounting Hall of Fame is because in his career he wrote close to thirty books on accounting. Most of them were academic and carried titles like *Management Control in Non-Profit Organizations*. I don't recommend that book to normal people. My grandfather generally wrote for people seeking deep expertise—people who really wanted to develop mastery over a subject. People who would take a year or two out of their career to enroll in an MBA program and study with an expert like my grandfather.

---

3. In 2001, I accompanied my grandfather to the American Association of Accountants meeting in Atlanta. His sight was failing him, so I was there to help him get around. People generally looked at him with the kind of awe that a rock star might receive. It was surreal and was the first time I realized the esteem with which my grandfather was held in his profession.

My grandfather built a nice business model for himself. He taught at an MBA program. He received royalties on his books. And he received fees from companies that wanted to draw upon his expertise.

But in the early 1960s, he had an insight. He was only reaching a very narrow group of customers—the expertise seekers. There was an entirely different—and substantially larger—market he was ignoring. This was the person who wanted to be conversant in accounting. Such a person didn't need to be an expert, but needed to know the meaning of the words on a financial statement.

My grandfather knew that having an impact on this audience would require something entirely different. In 1962, he introduced a book titled *Essentials of Accounting*. It differed sharply from his previous work. Instead of dense text to accompany expert instruction, *Essentials* was a do-it-yourself workbook. Readers could go through, fill in blanks, and learn by doing. By the end, they knew the difference between a debit and a credit. They knew common terms like *accounts receivable*. And they had a good sense of how to read basic financial statements.

The book, now in its tenth edition, has sold more than a million copies. That's not Steig Larsson, of course, but for an accounting book, that's pretty darn impressive.[4] My grandfather didn't sit still, either. Always an eager adopter of new

---

4. I'm betting that Larsson stays in pop culture for at least a few more years as Hollywood turns his books into movies. When I first started telling this story in 2005, I used John Grisham; by 2007, I was using the Harry Potter books. The world changes fast!

technologies, he introduced in the early 1980s a computer-based version of *Essentials*. One of the early beta testers was his then eight-year-old grandson (me).

My grandfather made accounting simple, accessible, and affordable. He reaped the benefits of innovation.

So too did Lizzie Jury. I learned about Jury when Innosight was doing work for Turner Broadcasting System, Inc., the cable broadcaster that owns CNN, TNT, TBS, Cartoon Network, and a range of other television channels.[5] In the mid-2000s, Jury was a senior librarian working for CNN. Her job was generally reactive. As journalists were developing their stories, they would contact her looking to verify specific facts on news topics.

She wondered if there was a better approach. What if she could be more anticipatory? She began assembling preverified facts on important topics in the news. She put these "Fast Facts" on the company intranet, making them instantly accessible to journalists.

Think about how this relatively straightforward move from being reactive to being proactive would help Turner Broadcasting. The improved process allowed journalists to verify facts more quickly, leading to more efficient news production. This could allow CNN to get stories on the air

---

5. One of my favorite moments was visiting Turner Broadcasting's corporate headquarters and seeing the World Series trophy from the Atlanta Braves' 1995 season (the team was owned by Turner Broadcasting at the time). I also had an unsuccessful quest to get a Ted Turner bobble-head doll. If you have one, let me know.

faster—always a critical factor in an industry where the rule of thumb is "faster than anyone better, better than anyone faster." The overall operational improvement would free up resources to pursue new opportunities, helping the company to create new growth.

Lizzie Jury made it easier for journalists to get the facts they needed. She reaped the benefits of innovation.

The third story turns back to my family and my older sister Michelle, who has a gift with children. She is the proud and doting mother of two girls and a boy, all of whom learned to sleep through the night at very young ages.[6] Through the years, she has received many requests from other young parents looking to sleep-train their children or, later, to accelerate the pace with which their children learn to read. My sister could easily have just responded to each request individually. But she started collecting and collating individual e-mail conversations. Then when someone e-mailed a new request, not only did the parent get a specific answer, but he or she also received my sister's "manual" for child rearing.[7] In business jargon, my sister crowd-sourced a peer-to-peer manual to minimize the frustration of young parents.

---

6. If you thought renowned pediatrician Dr. Ferber was tough, you should meet my sister. There is no wavering in the Anthony method. It is, however, quite effective. My sister, who provided tons of help on this book, made me promise to note that she is a good human being. She is.

7. Of course, my sister doesn't always tell people she plans to use their stories. Beware about giving Michelle personal details—because they *will* be shared with others!

My sister has helped hundreds of people more effectively raise their children. She—and her friends and family—reaped the benefits of innovation.

Types of Innovation

These three stories show how innovation comes in many guises. Just like the blogger who identified twenty-five ways to define innovation, there are dozens of ways to categorize innovation and hundreds of stories to tell. If you read the literature, you will see words like *incremental*, *radical*, *sustaining*, *disruptive*, *competency-creating*, and many, many more.

I find it helpful to look at innovation in one of two ways. The first is the innovation's *strategic intent*. Consider Procter & Gamble, the consumer packaged goods company responsible for Pampers, Pantene, Tide, Fusion, Ariel, and dozens of other megabrands. The company follows four strategic intents in its efforts to grow revenue:

- Find better ways to market and promote existing products. For example, in the mid-2000s, P&G started running a series of commercials about its popular Swiffer line of quick-cleaning products. The commercials, internally called the breakup campaign, showed women "breaking up" with traditional cleaning methods (mops, brooms, and so on) to use Swiffer. The intent was to show consumers that Swiffer wasn't just for quick cleans between "real" cleans, but a cleaning solution on its own. At the time only about 10 percent of consumers had ever tried Swiffer, and P&G hoped the advertisements would boost that rate. P&G calls this strategy *commercial* innovation.

- Incrementally improve existing products and services. You might think that one of the most challenging innovation jobs must be to discover new paths to growth for laundry detergent in North America. After all, the product is ubiquitous, and P&G's flagship Tide brand has dominated the market for years. But during the 2000s, P&G increased sales of Tide significantly by introducing dozens of new varieties of the detergent. Some of the varieties featured new scents; others combined Tide with other popular P&G products like Downy fabric softener. P&G calls this *sustaining* innovation. In P&G's language, these are the "-er" innovations (*better, faster, cheaper*).

- Introduce a breakthrough in performance in existing categories. In 2005, P&G purchased razor king Gillette for $57 billion.[8] P&G was impressed by Gillette's soon-to-be-launched Fusion razor and razor blade combination— the world's first five-blade razor (technically, it has six: five on its face and a sixth on the top for trimming). By offering sharply better performance, Gillette

---

8. The founder of Gillette was a gentleman named King Gillette. You see that clever word play? Just wait until you see what is coming in a few sentences.

increased its already substantial lead in the category.[9] The Fusion became the fastest brand in P&G's history to reach $1 billion in sales. P&G calls this kind of category step-change *transformational* innovation.

- Create a new category. In the late 1990s, P&G's household care division launched two new brands—Swiffer and Febreze. Swiffer in essence created the quick-clean category—a range of simple devices with disposable elements that made cleaning quick and easy. Febreze allowed consumers to remove odors in hard-to-clean fabrics such as carpets or couches and created new ways to deodorize and refresh the air in rooms. As of this book's writing, Swiffer's annual revenues had crossed $1 billion, with Febreze closing in on that magical ten-digit number. P&G calls this *disruptive innovation*.

The other way to categorize innovation is to look at the type of innovation. For example, Apple sometimes introduces new *products*, such as new versions of its music players, computers, or mobile devices. The company has also introduced new ways to *distribute* its products and associated content, like its iTunes music store or App Store for mobile phone applications. Apple has created entirely new *revenue models*, such as selling individual songs for low price points. Companies can innovate their *processes*, too, as Turner

---

9. Get it—sharply better performance. From a razor blade. Ha! I will try to not have two footnotes in a paragraph again.

Broadcasting did with its Fast Facts program. Big or small, all of these kinds of innovation are something different that had impact. And while there are plenty of examples of innovation that involve technology, many others involve ways to market, sell, promote, act, or organize.

Who Needs Innovation?

We often think that innovation really matters only to a small group of people, like corporate leaders steering their companies through changing industry conditions, entrepreneurs hoping to create the next big thing, and research scientists dutifully developing the technologies to enable both. But the innovation imperative is shared by all of us.

The sheer volume of self-help books, daily talk shows, executive coaches, and professional advisory firms suggest that people feel the need to change as they never have before. Perhaps that's not surprising, given how quickly our world seems to be changing today. Step back to the year 2000. There were no online social networks like Facebook and MySpace. In 2000, people largely communicated by e-mail and telephone. A few leading-edge users sent quick text messages to each other using their mobile phones, or via an instant-messaging software application. A few people had begun to capture their thoughts in online journals that today are called blogs. There certainly was no user-contributed video site, like Google's popular YouTube. Google itself was still in its infancy in 2000, with annual revenue of $19 million dollars (Google makes that much revenue in a few hours today). Apple was still Apple Computer, Inc., a niche player in the personal-computing market, with a market capitalization of about $3 billion (as opposed to today's $300 billion-plus). China, India, and Brazil were on the fringes of the world economy. If you wanted to read a book like this, then you bought, or were given . . . a thing . . . with physical pages. Today, many of you are probably reading this on a Kindle, an iPad, a Nook, an iPhone, or some other electronic device. Back then, the government was arguing that Microsoft was an unassailable monopoly that needed to be broken up (from January 1, 2000, to January 1, 2010, Microsoft's stock declined by close to 40 percent). The United States was a hegemonic superpower that could enjoy its "peace dividend" as a result of the "victory" in the Cold War. The world has changed a tremendous amount in a decade.

While it's very hard to know for sure what the future holds, technology continues to advance at a rapid clip. Economic or political shocks might reverse a seventy-year trend toward more closely connected markets, but it is hard to imagine emerging economies stepping *off* the world stage. Certainly, the continued rise of communications technologies will make distributed collaboration and communication easier.

We all have to deal with innovation. In his 1996 book *Only the Paranoid Survive*, legendary Intel Corporation CEO Andy Grove put it well: "Strategic inflection points offer promises as well as threats. It is at such times of fundamental change that the cliché 'adapt or die' takes on its true meaning." The increasing pace of change means that these times of fundamental change are ever present; the new normal is perpetual change.

This change places two levels of stress on each of us. First, the companies at which we work need to adapt. Consider these statistics. During my parents' lifetime, the life expectancy in wealthy countries has increased by about 33 percent, from sixty to eighty years. During that same time, the life expectancy of large, successful corporations, by some measures, has been cut in half, from roughly forty years to roughly twenty years.[10] Think about what that means. A generation ago, you very well could have been working for the same company your parents worked for, and you might hope to have your kids work there as well. Today, if you work for a large, successful company, the odds are your parents didn't work there, and your kids probably will never have heard of the company, because by the time they enter the workforce, the company will have stumbled or been acquired. The only way to buck those odds is to innovate.

Many companies I advised in the midst of the 2008–2009 downturn told me they thought they had a choice—bet on innovation and growth, or curtail growth efforts in order to

---

10. The corporate life-expectancy figure is based on research done by Richard Foster (discussed in more detail in the next chapter). Foster analyzed the annual turnover in the S&P 500 index, whose five hundred committee-selected members cover about 75 percent of the market capitalization of U.S. equity markets. In his 2001 book *Creative Destruction*, Foster found that the turnover had been increasing steadily over the past sixty years. We updated the analysis in August 2010. Up until the 1960s, the average turnover was running about 2 to 3 percent (corresponding to a forty- to fifty-year life span). Today, that figure is about 5 to 6 percent (corresponding to a fifteen- to twenty-year life span).

survive. In today's world, innovation is not a choice. If you do not innovate, you are sowing the seeds of your own destruction. Success requires waking up every day and realizing that today's sources of competitive advantage will not be tomorrow's; that the products or services that constitute the core of today's business might not constitute the core of tomorrow's business; that success might require walking away from the things that you view as your core competency.

That's all well and good for companies, but there are equal stresses on individuals. Organizations only adapt if their employees adapt. That means each of us needs to think not just about how we do today's job better, but about how we change and redefine the tasks that we do. And we have to do this not just in our job, but at home as well. We must learn to adapt to new means of communication between family members. To prepare our children for the hypercompetitive world they are entering. And on and on.

The individual implications of innovation hit home to me when we were looking for Christmas presents for our then three-year-old daughter Holly. My wife suggested getting her a Dora the Explorer toy laptop to encourage her interest in technology. Holly loved the laptop, but she more frequently picked up and interacted with our Apple iPad and played with our Microsoft Kinect. Watching Holly reinforced my belief that the odds that the laptop will be the dominant means of accessing technology by the time Holly enters the workforce are close to zero.

We all have to come to grips with the reality of an increasingly dynamic world. I'm willing to bet that all of you do

Holly, enjoying her Dora the Explorer laptop.

your job in some kind of different way than you did when you started working. Look at the seemingly prosaic world of consulting. I joined McKinsey & Company as an analyst in 1996. My colleagues and I received training on how to place acetates on overhead projectors during presentations. There was an art to the practice of managing voicemail.[11] One of my managers told me that one source of competitive advantage was our library, where we had stacks of paper reports that were too expensive for individual companies to purchase. We could pore over those reports to find critical data that our clients couldn't obtain.

That wasn't so long ago. And it is a safe bet that more will change in the industry in the next fifteen years as technology advances, collaborative networks and emerging markets rise

---

11. One colleague became a legend for figuring out how to get the Audix system to time-stamp a message so that it appeared as though she was working insane hours.

in importance, and entrepreneurs craft innovative consulting models.

Innovation is *the* imperative of today's times. We all have to learn to be comfortable with change so that we can do the job that awaits us in the next few years, communicate with our colleagues, and provide the best guidance to our children and other loved ones. We all have to be innovators.

What image enters your head when you read the word *innovators*? When I ask people who they consider innovators, they typically think of icons like Apple's Steve Jobs, Virgin Group's Sir Richard Branson, or Facebook founder Mark Zuckerberg.

No doubt that these people are fantastic innovators. But I suggest that if you want to see someone with a great capacity to innovate, you should amble over to the mirror. Have a look. Yup. That's you.

Why Innovation Is Attainable

There are three reasons why I believe that innovation is within anyone's grasp. First, the so-called masters of innovation who we'll meet in the next chapter have done a great job unearthing patterns and principles that help bring clarity to the formerly fuzzy world of innovation. Putting those patterns to work can allow anyone to markedly improve his or her innovation skills.

Second, an important change is taking place in the world of innovation. Put simply, innovation can be done very cheaply. It used to be that innovation was relatively expensive.

For example, one case taught in Harvard Business School's entrepreneurship program describes how Robin Wolaner came up with an idea in the mid-1980s for a high-quality magazine targeting parents. Wolaner's original plan suggested that it would cost $5 million to develop the idea. Before she attempted to raise that amount of capital, she decided to run a simple market test. She sent a sample issue of her magazine to a set of parents. Each test issue included a reply card that people could return to indicate interest in subscribing. High levels of response validated the market interest in the idea, and Wolaner was off and running. She eventually sold her magazine (*Parenting*) to Time Life, Inc., for about $10 million. This test cost Wolaner about $150,000 to run.

Contrast Wolaner's story to the two bright entrepreneurs my colleague and I met in Singapore in September 2010. The duo had an idea for a Web site that would democratize tools used by designers of a type of chip called a field programmable gate array (FPGA). It's a big market—the companies that sell FPGAs are multibillion-dollar enterprises, and the leading tool providers are big companies, too. The founders had built a functional Web site with real, live tools. They had run a marketing campaign to attract a couple hundred users to the site. The company had earned modest revenues.

"Wow," we said. "A functional Web site, a marketing campaign, and early revenue. Who are your investors, and how much have they invested to date?"

They looked at each other sheepishly. The total out-of-pocket investment was less than $1,000. They had done the Web site themselves in their spare time. They did focused advertising on Google to attract early customers. Now *that's* what I call doing things on the cheap!

If Wolaner was launching her magazine business today (perhaps a dubious proposal in the current media market), there is simply no way she would need to spend $150,000 running tests. You could probably run the same set of tests for less than $5,000 using primarily free or easily available tools on the Internet.[12]

The low cost of innovation affects all of us by giving us more options. Think about weight loss. Instead of just relying on willpower or going to a specialist weight-loss clinic, innovators have given us an incredible variety of dieting applications in Apple's App Store. One application allows you to take pictures of everything you eat in a given day to get a reasonable assessment of your caloric intake. Or you can buy small, wearable devices connected to online services that show how much exercise you did in a given day, with a whole community of weight-loss seekers supporting you. Further, scientists increasingly throw out new mechanisms to lose weight, with ideas transmitted in a blink of an eye on Facebook, Twitter, and other networking tools.

The third reason that innovation is achievable is that the specific traits and behaviors common to successful innovators are coming into sharper focus. Do you think successful innovators

---

12. My favorite low-cost tools are Google SketchUp (for design), SurveyMonkey (to gather data), Skype (for communications), LinkedIn (to find industry experts), eLance.com (a tool that helps you find individual contractors), Wix.com (for designing Web sites), Google AdWords (for targeted marketing), and legalzoom.com (for basic legal services). There are tons more.

are different in some meaningful way? Most people would answer that question with an emphatic yes. But academics struggled for a long time to isolate those differences. A recent stream of research by Jeffrey Dyer from Brigham Young University, Hal Gregersen from INSEAD, and Clayton Christensen from Harvard decodes the innovator's DNA. The professors found that a successful innovator is good at what they call *associational thinking*. That is, good innovators make connections between seemingly unconnected inputs. Watch HBO's hit show *Entourage* to see associational thinking in action. It takes ten seconds for the character Ari Gold and the other agents to describe screenplays they are considering. They don't go through long descriptions of the plot. Instead, they offer a short summary with an anchor analogy (what this movie resembles) and a twist (what makes it novel). For instance, the movie *Speed* with Keanu Reeves was pitched as "*Die Hard* on a bus." Imagine hearing that pitch. You'd say, "*Die Hard*. Huh. That was a pretty successful movie. On a bus. Haven't heard that one before. That might be interesting." In their book *Made to Stick*, Chip and Dan Heath dubbed this technique the *Hollywood pitch*.

Sounds great, but can you improve your own associational thinking? The professors describe how successful innovators follow four time-tested approaches to gather stimuli so they can make these connections:

- Questioning: asking probing questions that impose or remove constraints (e.g., what if we were legally prohibited from selling to our current customer?)

- Networking: interacting with people from different backgrounds and who provide access to new ways of thinking

- Observing: watching the world around yourself for surprising stimuli

- Experimenting: consciously complicating your life by trying new things or going to new places

There's nothing here that you can't do. My twenty-eight-day innovation program, detailed in part 2, provides further tricks of the trade to help you develop these and other innovation capabilities.

The larger point is that the innovation potential is in all of us. The next chapter, which provides key lessons from a select group of masters of innovation, can help you begin to realize that potential.

CHAPTER 2

THE MASTERS OF INNOVATION

From Blank to Schumpeter: a short list
of innovation inspiration

A search for the word *innovation* on a random Wednesday
on Amazon returned more than forty-one thousand books.
Let's assume that you are a fast reader and can get through
each of these books in two days. Reading through these
books, then, would take 225 years.

This chapter aims to give you at least some of those years
back by providing key lessons from select sources—twelve
so-called masters of innovation. These experts bring great
clarity to the field of innovation (summarized in table 2-1).
The appendix provides additional recommended reading.

A few caveats before getting into substance. First, this isn't
an academically sanctioned review of the innovation literature—some of the people mentioned below don't officially
focus on innovation. There is a bias to people who present

TABLE 2-1

The masters of innovation

Master	Seminal work	Key innovation lesson
Steve Blank	*The Four Steps to the Epiphany*	A start-up is a temporary organization searching for a scalable business model; a structured search process maximizes your chances of success.
Clayton Christensen	*The Innovator's Solution*	Doing everything right can leave a successful organization susceptible to attack from a disruptive innovator that changes the game with a simple, accessible, or affordable solution.
Peter Drucker	*Innovation and Entrepreneurship*	"The customer rarely buys what the company thinks it is selling him." Companies need to take a customer-first perspective to succeed with innovation.
Thomas Alva Edison	The incandescent light bulb	"Genius is 1 percent inspiration and 99 percent perspiration." If you aren't sweating, you aren't innovating.
Richard N. Foster	*Creative Destruction*	To outperform the market, you have to change at the pace and scale of the market, without losing control.
Vijay Govindarajan	*Ten Rules for Strategic Innovators*	Existing companies that want to master strategic innovation have to carefully borrow some core capabilities, thoughtfully forget others, and systematically learn some completely new skills.
Bill James	*The New Bill James Historical Abstract*	Looking at old data in new ways can highlight counterintuitive patterns that overthrow orthodoxy.
A. G. Lafley	*The Game-Changer*	Innovation is a process that can be managed and measured; the key to successful innovation is a consumer-is-boss mind-set.
Roger Martin	*The Design of Business*	Managers increasingly need to take *or*s and turn them into *and*s.

Master	Seminal work	Key innovation lesson
Michael Mauboussin	*More Than You Know*	Breakthrough insight can come from applying lessons from nonobvious fields to your problem.
Rita McGrath	*Discovery-Driven Growth*	Your first idea is wrong, so implement a careful plan to learn as quickly as possible which of your assumptions are flawed.
Joseph Schumpeter	*Capitalism, Socialism, and Democracy*	"The problem that is usually being visualized is how capitalism administers existing structures, whereas the relevant problem is how it creates and destroys them." Sometimes you have to destroy in order to create.

their findings accessibly. That, no doubt, shortchanges many influential academics.[1] Four hundred words obviously can't do justice to what each of these individuals teaches. Finally, the sources here admittedly lean toward Western voices that write and speak in English. But this summary is a good primer on some of the key voices in and around the field, and it provides critical grounding to help you adopt the right mind-sets (chapter 3), avoid pitfalls (chapter 4), and embark on the twenty-eight-day innovation program (part 2).

---

1. For example, the field wouldn't be where it is today without the historical contributions of academics like Henry Mintzberg, Robert Burgelman, Michael Tushman, James Utterback, C. K. Prahalad, Gary Hamel, Joseph Bower, W. Chan Kim, and Renée Mauborgne; more recent research by Constantinos C. Markides, Ron Adner, Jeffrey Dyer, Hal Gregersen, C. C. Hang, and Don Sull; and writings of leading-edge practitioners like Larry Doblin and Geoffrey Moore.

Steve Blank (1953–)

Who he is: Seasoned entrepreneur who lectures at Berkeley and Stanford (www.steveblank.com)

If you read one book, read: *The Four Steps to the Epiphany* (Cafepress.com, 2005)

His most important innovation lesson: A start-up is a "temporary organization searching for a repeatable and scalable business model"—a structured search process maximizes your chances of success.

A colleague pointed me toward Steve Blank's writing in early 2010. After reading one blog post, I was hooked. Blank has serious entrepreneurial chops. He worked at Convergent Technology, Zilog, and many other successful start-ups and played a role in starting E.piphany, Mips Computers, Ardent, and Rocket Science Games. Unlike many entrepreneurs who distill their success to a simple formula of "I'm smarter and work harder than you," Blank had his eye out for a systematic way to manage the creation of new ventures.

Blank's *The Four Steps to the Epiphany* summarizes his guidance. He tells innovators that their first plan is sure to be wrong. As a result, innovators should follow a disciplined process of "customer discovery," in which they get into the market as quickly as possible with what Blank calls a "minimal viable product." Selling that product to customers helps innovators learn *how* their plan is wrong. The key to success, Blank argues, is for innovators to use marketplace feedback to change their plan, or, in Blank's words, "to do a pivot."

One of Blank's key disciples is Eric Ries, who has further built out Blank's concepts by developing a complementary set of ideas captured in what Ries calls the "lean start-up." Ries borrows from the concepts of *agile development*, a technique that emerged over the past decade to manage the creation of new software programs. The basic concept is to rapidly release new versions of software and improve that software according to market feedback. The lean start-up tries to shorten the time between Blank's pivots. Blank's writing is lucid, practical, and often entertaining.

Clayton Christensen (1952–)

Who he is: Harvard Business School professor and Innosight cofounder (www.claytonchristensen.com)

If you read one book, read: *The Innovator's Solution*, with Michael E. Raynor (Harvard Business School Press, 2003)

His most important innovation lesson: Doing everything right can leave a successful organization susceptible to attack from a disruptive innovator who changes the game with a simple, accessible, or affordable solution.

Like many of the people on this list, Christensen lives at the intersections. Before becoming an academic, he had a successful career as a consultant (for the Boston Consulting Group) and a business leader (serving as the CEO of a start-up advanced-material company that raised millions in venture capital).

He is remarkably persistent. In 2002, I started two projects with Christensen to apply his research to the education and health-care industries. The original aim was to produce books on both of these industries by 2003. By early 2003, it was clear that the deadline wasn't even close to realistic. Christensen persevered, however, and the books (with different coauthors) came out in early 2009.

He's also probably the nicest human being you will ever meet. A consummate storyteller, Christensen has a gift of being able to spot patterns and formulate theories and frameworks that bring great clarity to a range of growth- and innovation-related challenges.

He is best known for his concept of disruptive innovation, which formed the backbone of his first and still most cited book, *The Innovator's Dilemma*. The book—described by then Intel CEO Andy Grove as "lucid, analytical, and scary"—argued that the roots of failure for many large companies were the principles of *good* management. Companies would do everything they were supposed to—listen to their best customers, innovate to meet their needs, produce the best products on the market, charge high prices, and enjoy soaring stock prices—and get caught off guard when a seemingly irrelevant competitor changed the game with a disruptive innovation that drove industry transformation through simplicity or affordability.

Christensen's fingerprints are on many other key innovation concepts. He has argued eloquently that business researchers should be trying to advance good theory. That is, they should develop robust categorization schemes of the circumstances facing managers and develop causal statements that predict how certain actions lead to certain results. I recommend *The Innovator's Solution* over *The Innovator's Dilemma* and Christensen's half-dozen other books, because the *Solution* tightly recaps the *Dilemma* in its second chapter and lays out the foundation for the work done by many practitioners in the 2000s.

Peter Drucker (1909–2005)

Who he is: Legendary management guru and longtime professor at the Claremont Graduate University

If you read one book, read: *Innovation and Entrepreneurship* (HarperCollins, 1985)

His most important innovation lesson: "The customer rarely buys what the company thinks it is selling him."

Companies need to take a customer-first perspective to succeed with innovation.

Peter Drucker is generally acknowledged as the most influential management thinker of the last century. Key to his influence was an uncanny ability to bring piercing clarity to a variety of topics. He was quite prescient, too, identifying, among other things, the rise of knowledge workers in a postindustrial economy. His old writing holds up remarkably well. Just look at some of these choice quotes:

- "The purpose of a business is to create a customer."

- "The customer rarely buys what the business thinks it is selling him."

- "The best way to predict the future is to create it."

- "Plans are only good intentions unless they immediately degenerate into hard work."

My favorite Drucker quote (the second on the list above) actually predates his focused writing on innovation by about twenty years. His seminal innovation work was the 1985 book *Innovation and Entrepreneurship*. In that book, Drucker argued that innovation could be a purposeful act. Drucker summarized the book in a classic *Harvard Business Review* article titled "The Discipline of Innovation." The penultimate paragraph is classic Drucker—clearly written, but noticeably different from prevailing mind-sets: "In innovation, as in any other endeavor, there is talent, there is ingenuity, and there is knowledge. But when all is said and done, what innovation requires is hard, focused, purposeful work.

If diligence, persistence, and commitment are lacking, talent, ingenuity, and knowledge are of no avail."

Drucker's thinking has spread in many ways. The personal coaching he provided another person on this list of innovation masters—A. G. Lafley—helped inform Lafley's quest to bring predictability to innovation at Procter & Gamble. You can even buy calendars that give you your daily dose of Drucker. I'm sorry I never got the chance to meet this man, who passed away at the age of ninety-five in 2005.

Thomas Alva Edison (1847–1931)

Who he is: Legendary innovator, credited with creating the light bulb, the phonograph, and other innovations

If you read one book, read: *The Wizard of Menlo Park: How Thomas Alva Edison Invented the Modern World*, by Randall E. Stross (Crown, 2007)

His most important innovation lesson: "Genius is 1 percent inspiration and 99 percent perspiration." If you aren't sweating, you aren't innovating.

Edison is clearly an inspiration for modern-day innovators like Steve Jobs and Richard Branson. Of course, much of Edison's life has now descended into myths that bear decreasing resemblance to reality, but every innovator should study the basic way he went about his work. So seminal are his contributions that I'll keep it brief here. In the next chapter, I'll describe how innovators need to release their inner Edison.

Richard N. Foster (1941–)

Who he is: The leading light on innovation at McKinsey & Company for two decades, now serving on a variety of boards (including Innosight's) and teaching at the Yale School of Management

If you read one book, read: *Creative Destruction*, with Sarah Kaplan (Currency/Doubleday, 2001)

His most important innovation lesson: To outperform the market, you have to change at the pace and scale of the market, without losing control.

I remember my first meeting with Dick Foster. It was a late afternoon in 2006 in Innosight's offices in Watertown, Massachusetts. I was a bit awestruck. When I was an analyst at McKinsey in the mid-1990s, Foster's name would be spoken in hushed terms. Not only was he an intellectual dynamo, but he also led the firm's relationship with one of its most important clients, a large, diversified health-care company.[2]

I had read both of his books (his first book carried the wonderful title of *Innovation: The Attacker's Advantage*) and knew of his contributions to the field of innovation. In his first book in the mid-1980s, Foster introduced the notion of technological S-curves. The simple notion is that if you drew a chart with cumulative time on the horizontal axis and technological progress on the vertical access, almost any technology would have a chart that looked like an *S*. It would take time for scientists to figure out the technology the chart tracked, so early development would be slow. Then it would inflect, and development would come rapidly. Importantly, it would then inflect again and development would again slow. Foster used this and other frameworks to show why attackers typically had the upper hand when it came to innovation. His research laid the foundation for Christensen's work a decade later.

Creative Destruction used a large sample database to argue that any company hoping to outperform the market has to change at the pace and scale of the market, without losing control. Foster found, counterintuitively, that long-term survivors (which he called "operators") underperformed the market, because markets created new things and disposed of (in Foster's language, "traded") old things.

---

2. McKinsey trains people to never reveal the names of their clients. So everyone at or around McKinsey knows precisely which company this is—Foster even names it in *Creative Destruction*. But I'll hold to the code and force you to look it up if you would like to.

Foster is intensely intellectually curious. If you ever meet him, ask him who made Brunelleschi's dome, and be prepared for a fascinating two-hour discussion on creativity.

Vijay Govindarajan (1949–)

Who he is: Tuck School of Business at Dartmouth Administration professor (www.vijaygovindarajan.com)

If you read one book, read: *Ten Rules for Strategic Innovators*, with Chris Trimble (Harvard Business School Press, 2005)

His most important innovation lesson: Existing companies that want to master "strategic" innovation have to carefully borrow some core capabilities, thoughtfully forget others, and systematically learn selected new skills.

I first met Govindarajan at a conference in 2004. He looked me up and down and said, "You aren't related to *Bob* Anthony, are you?" Turns out that my grandfather served as a source of inspiration that led Govindarajan to apply to Harvard's MBA program. The two ultimately coauthored several accounting books (including the scintillating *Management Control Systems*). If you ever have the opportunity to hear Govindarajan speak, take it. He and

Christensen are the two best speakers on this list. Like Christensen, Govindarajan is a genuinely nice guy.[3]

Over the past decade, Govindarajan has primarily focused on how corporations can manage what he calls "strategic," or "Box 3" innovations, which involve creating new markets or targeting new customers. He notes how important it is for strategic innovators to carefully manage how they interact with the core business, because the core "DNA" can sometimes run counter to what innovators are trying to accomplish. Govindarajan guides innovators to thoughtfully forget some pieces of that DNA, selectively borrow others, and learn to fill in the cracks.

Govindarajan has recently written about other important concepts. In 2009, he wrote a *Harvard Business Review* article (with Chris Trimble and General Electric chairman Jeffrey Immelt) that introduced the term *reverse innovation*. The article, titled "How GE Is Disrupting Itself," urged companies to move from viewing branches in emerging markets as vehicles to distribute Western-developed products to developing market-appropriate products locally. In 2010, Govindarajan and Trimble released *The Other Side of Innovation*, which details execution. Both the article and the book are worthwhile reads.

---

3. You know, everyone on this list and with whom I've had the fortune of interacting comes across as a good human being. It reminds me of a theory that Bill James advanced about baseball players. The defensive wizards like Ozzie Smith and Brooks Robinson have reputations as affable, good-natured people. Hitting specialists like Ted Williams, Barry Bonds, and Albert Belle have reputations as self-centered jerks. James argued that any player whose biggest strength is their defense knows that he only succeeds by having great teammates, so he becomes a great teammate. Perhaps there's something about the field of innovation and its focus on creation that attracts the right sort of people.

Bill James (1949–)

Who he is: Baseball writer, historian, and senior adviser to the Boston Red Sox (www.billjamesonline.net)

If you read one book, read: *The New Bill James Historical Abstract* (Free Press, 2001)

His most important innovation lesson: Looking at old data in new ways can highlight counterintuitive patterns that overthrow orthodoxy.

James is probably the least obvious person on this list. But the way he has brought insight to the baseball diamond has important lessons for innovators. I have always been a baseball fan.[4] In fact, my mother suggests that any acuity I have

---

4. My family had season tickets to the Orioles between 1984 and 1998. By my count, I've been to more than five hundred baseball games. Some key memories include two World Series (1983, 2007), four league championship series (1983, 1997, 1998, 2008), two no-hitters (Juan Nieves and Wilson Alvarez), the games where Cal Ripken Jr. tied and broke Lou Gehrig's consecutive game streak, the last game at Memorial Stadium, the first game at Camden Yards, and the August 24, 1983, game where Tippy Martinez picked off three overeager base runners in one inning. (Truth be told, I listened to the end of the game on the radio because staying to the end of the game would have been a bit much for an eight-year-old! See www.retrosheet.org/boxesetc/1983/B08240BAL1983.htm for the details.)

around mathematics comes from learning how to quickly calculate batting averages.

Bill James began writing an annual book called *The Bill James Baseball Abstract* in 1977. In those books, he would present a raft of nontraditional statistics, like situational performance, and write essays that used statistics to provide a fresh perspective on the common wisdom that had ruled the game for decades. I got my first copy of *The Bill James Abstract* in the mid-1980s, and it nearly caused my ten-year-old head to explode. Sure, much of James's writing went well over my head, but I couldn't miss that this was someone who was debunking much of the conventional wisdom in baseball.

James was on the cutting edge of a field known as sabermetrics, which is named after the Society of American Baseball Research. The findings from these research efforts have overturned orthodoxy and influenced in-game tactics, investment decisions, and personnel management. James is not the most academically pure or statistically minded of the sabermetricians, but he combines great instincts with a compelling writing style. His work was the inspiration for my 2009 *Harvard Business Review* article "Major League Innovation."[5]

James's work is applicable to innovation because the essence of what he and other sabermetricians do is what innovation scholars seek to do. These researchers look for patterns and data that bring greater predictability to questions such as

---

5. HBR did a great job massaging my 5,000-word piece into a tight 2,300 words. If you are interested in the full treatment, feel free to shoot me an e-mail at santhony@innosight.com.

these: What exactly is it that creates value? Which statistics are most meaningful? Which statistics result from skill versus luck or other extraneous factors? Which strategies actually create value, and which do not? Just as James and his colleagues have driven a revolution in baseball, so have the other people on this list laid the foundation for a revolution in innovation.

A. G. Lafley (1947–)

Who he is: Former chairman and CEO of Procter & Gamble

If you read one book, read: *The Game-Changer*, with Ram Charan (Crown Business, 2008)

His most important innovation lesson: Innovation is a process that can be managed and measured; the key to successful innovation is a "consumer is boss" mind-set.

I met Lafley in 2008 at a newspaper industry conference in Washington, D.C., where he was participating in a panel discussion I was facilitating. The topic was transformation. Then presidential candidate Barack Obama had visited the previous day, with the "neutral" journalists still buzzing about his charisma and charm.[6] I knew P&G well from working with various parts of the company over the past few years, but only knew Lafley by reputation. Lafley had just released his book, and after the panel discussion, he asked if I wouldn't mind joining him at a few more events throughout the year to promote the book's messages because he enjoyed the talk-show-style discussion format. I happily accepted.

Lafley's core message is that innovation should be treated in a disciplined way. That message has teeth from someone who is widely credited with transforming P&G from a stodgy household staples company into a vibrant health and beauty company. Further, one of Lafley's great gifts is explaining complicated concepts in simple-to-understand terms—he calls it "Sesame Street simple" after the popular U.S. television program aimed at toddlers and preschoolers. His book is a wonderful description of how P&G approaches innovation. I regularly refer to my notes from our discussion at the Front End of Innovation conference in Boston in May 2008.[7] The details of the consumer-is-boss approach described later in the book are ripped straight from Lafley's stump speech.

To repeat a theme, Lafley comes across as a genuine, down-to-earth guy. After one event in Arizona, we attended

---

6. Hillary Clinton spoke at lunch the day I was there. The journalists buzzed about the chicken that was served.

7. You can see a recap of the event at Scott D. Anthony, "Game-Changing at Procter & Gamble," *Strategy & Innovation* 6, no. 4 (July–August 2008), www.innosight.com/documents/protected/SI/JulyAugust2008StrategyandInnovation.pdf.

a dinner party at the home of P&G's then head of external relations. Since it was a weekend, I had brought my wife and son Charlie, who was two years old at the time. My host was about to show Charlie a small toy tractor that her grandkids liked to play with when Lafley arrived. Lafley immediately left the party to follow Charlie outside and watch him ride the tractor, his face beaming with excitement.[8]

Roger Martin (1956–)

Who he is: Dean of the Rotman School of Management, University of Toronto

If you read one book, read: *The Design of Business* (Harvard Business Press, 2009)

His most important innovation lesson: Managers increasingly need to take *or*s and turn them into *and*s.

Martin comes across as very thoughtful. Consequently, it is probably not a surprise that he ended up in Toronto. To generalize a bit, the U.S. East Coast is the home of structured

---

8. Perhaps that was because we had trained Charlie to greet Lafley by saying, "Thank you for my diapers," which my son dutifully did!

strategy, the kind espoused by Michael Porter and colleagues at Harvard Business School. The U.S. West Coast is the home of dynamic entrepreneurialism and, increasingly, design thinking typified by Stanford's Hasso Plattner Institute of Design (called the d.school) and IDEO. Martin sits intellectually (if not quite geographically) between these two poles.

His mission is to live at the intersections, helping managers to integrate different schools of thought. His training came from the Monitor Company, which in the 1980s and early 1990s was *the* place to be if you wanted to intersect academic research and applied consulting. Since becoming dean of Rotman in 1998, Martin has worked to create a unique position for himself and his school. Martin's first book, *The Opposable Mind*, argued that executives increasingly had to develop the mental acuity to deal with seemingly paradoxical demands (a notion picked up and developed further by Cisco executive Inder Sidhu in his 2010 book, *Doing Both*). In *The Design of Business*, Martin made the compelling case that the principles of design thinking could be powerful tools in the strategist's arsenal.

Martin isn't a pure theoretician. He created an organization at Rotman called DesignWorks, which essentially provides business design services to companies. In 2009, I worked with a Procter & Gamble team that had worked with a student team from DesignWorks. The output from the student team was as good as anything produced by a top-tier innovation specialist. With his clear, distinct perspective on strategy and innovation, Martin is worth following closely.

Michael Mauboussin (1964–)

Who he is: Chief investment strategist at Legg Mason (www.michaelmauboussin.com)

If you read one book, read: *More Than You Know* (Columbia University Press, 2007)

His most important innovation lesson: Breakthrough insight can come from applying lessons from nonobvious fields to your problem.

I had heard about Mauboussin in glowing terms from Christensen before meeting him at a 2004 conference. He is a fascinating guy. Like Martin, he straddles the intersections. By day he is an investment strategist for a company controlling billions in assets. By night he is a scholar, affiliated with the Santa Fe Institute and an adjunct faculty member at Columbia University since 1993.

Mauboussin has the rare ability to pick up an academic idea that seems to have nothing to do with finance and spin a cogent analysis of the concept's implication for strategists and investors. One of my favorite chapters in *More Than You Know* talked about how the Colonel Blotto game (and you aren't alone if you don't know what that is) provides useful insights for financial investors. Mauboussin takes on provocative topics, such as, Can a company actually influence the makeup of its shareholders? Is persistence in investment outperformance real? Is investment luck or skill?[9] When I once asked him what he read, he named the *New York Times*, *The Economist*, the *Wall Street Journal*, *Fortune*, *Nature*, *Scientific America*, and the legion of articles that fans and friends send to him.

Rita McGrath (1959–)

Who she is: Columbia University professor (www. ritamcgrath. com)

If you read one book, read: *Discovery-Driven Growth*, with Ian MacMillan (Harvard Business Press, 2009)

Her most important innovation lesson: Your first idea is wrong, so, as quickly as possible, implement a careful plan to learn which of your assumptions are flawed.

---

9. You really should read Mauboussin to get the answers, but in short, he suggests that the answers to those three questions are, respectively, yes a company can influence its shareholder set; persistence exists, but barely; and investment performance is mostly (but not entirely) luck.

McGrath looks like a serious academic. She publishes in academic journals, attends high-minded affairs like the annual Davos conference, and is a well-regarded teacher at Columbia University's executive education program. But she "speaks practitioner." The books she writes with her long-term collaborator Ian MacMillan of Wharton are filled with simple, helpful tools. For example, if you go to the companion Web site for *Discovery-Driven Growth*, you can download a tool called the BareBones NPV, which allows you to create a thumbnail financial projection for your business idea.

McGrath counsels innovators to always start with an answer and then to work backward to map out assumptions that would need to be true for that answer to be plausible. Develop a discovery-driven plan, she says, to test the most critical assumptions. Be prepared to adjust the plan according to what you learn. This approach can end up dramatically accelerating innovation. McGrath also guides leaders to think strategically about innovation. She has a simple template to capture the different ideas that constitute a company's growth portfolio. Working through the template almost always sparks fantastic strategic discussions.

McGrath's writing illustrates the wide-ranging applicability of her ideas, drawing on examples from *Fortune* 500 companies, small local businesses, and personal life. For a shorter treatment of the topic, check out her and MacMillan's 1995 *Harvard Business Review* article "Discovery-Driven Planning." It is a classic.

Joseph Schumpeter (1883–1950)

Who he is: Austrian economist

If you read one book, read: *Capitalism, Socialism, and Democracy* (Harper & Brothers, 1942)

His most important innovation lesson: "The problem that is usually being visualized is how capitalism administers existing structures, whereas the relevant problem is how it creates and destroys them"; sometimes you have to destroy in order to create.

We live in an interconnected world. Schumpeter is widely credited for coining the term *creative destruction*, which became the name of Richard Foster's 2001 book. Schumpeter was friends with Peter Drucker's father. Drucker, along with Roger Martin, ended up being a personal adviser to A. G. Lafley, who graduated from Harvard Business School the same year Clayton Christensen entered HBS. Whew!

Schumpeter was the intellectual father of the study of innovation. Unlike so-called neoclassical economists, he presented his work largely free of complicated mathematical equations. His seminal book was, in fact, an academic argument about different economic systems. Schumpeter argued that entrepreneurs who unleashed the power of creative destruction kept large companies that might abuse their market power in check. This creative destruction, he argued, was what made capitalism such a powerful model. Whereas most economists focused on Adam Smith's so-called invisible hand that balanced supply and demand, Schumpeter talked about how innovation was the most important force for change in a market and society. Most people connect innovation with creation—Schumpeter forces people to think about destruction as well.

My intention in introducing you to these masters of innovation was to highlight key innovation lessons and to point out where you could go to learn more. The next two chapters summarize the lessons and warnings from these masters and from my own personal innovation journey.

CHAPTER 3

THE MOUNT RUSHMORE OF INNOVATION

Four faces to guide your innovation efforts

This chapter and the next one round out the foundational section of this book by describing key mind-sets that can increase your chances of successful innovation and highlighting a handful of pitfalls to avoid. Each chapter organizes key points around a central metaphor. Then part 2 details more specific guidance about how to tactically use these mind-sets and avoid these pitfalls.

Let's start with what you *should* do. Want to do something different that has impact? Look to the four faces chiseled onto the Mount Rushmore of Innovation: (from left) A. G. Lafley, Robert N. Anthony Sr., Thomas Edison, and Mike Tyson.

Brian Lazar

A. G. Lafley (Take an External Viewpoint)

If you ask people within Procter & Gamble the most important thing innovation master A. G. Lafley imprinted on the
company during his decade as leader, odds are they will
respond with, "The consumer is boss." Lafley used this
mantra to urge P&G to get out into the market to understand
current and prospective customers in more depth, to understand not just what they were saying, but also what they
were feeling or unable to articulate. Lafley's face on the
Mount Rushmore of Innovation reminds us to always take
an external viewpoint that draws inspiration from outside
sources.

The most obvious way in which an external viewpoint is
valuable is in the identification of opportunities. Companies
often look for opportunities by saying something along the
lines of, "We have these things to sell. Who wants to buy

them?" An externally oriented company starts by saying, "What does the customer want or need?" Innovation master Peter Drucker explained the wisdom of this external orientation when he noted, "The customer rarely buys what the business thinks it sells him . . . Nobody pays for a 'product.' What is paid for is satisfaction." A company might *think* it sells products or provides services, but the customer doesn't look at the world that way. The customer has a problem to solve or a job to get done.

Spotting problems not yet solved or jobs not yet done requires looking at the situation from the outside in. Spending time with your target—whether that target is a current customer, a prospective one, your spouse, a trouble-causing co-worker, or a backyard bully—is the best way to develop the empathy that can allow you to understand what the person says he or she wants and needs and, even more importantly, what the person actually wants and needs but can't easily articulate.

This externally derived empathy also helps to avoid common innovation mistakes. Innovators often think that their personal preferences overlap with their customers' preferences. Or they think the hardest things to do are what customers will value most. The customer might very well prefer something simple and affordable over more complex but higher-performing solutions, or might be seeking performance along a dimension that doesn't matter to you. Just think of how Nintendo succeeded in the video game industry with its easy-to-use Wii console, or the millions of hours people spend playing *Mafia Wars* and

Farmville on their Facebook accounts. There are always customers looking for bleeding-edge performance, but many prefer easy-to-use solutions.

An external viewpoint helps with two additional innovation challenges: formulating compelling new ideas and choosing between alternatives with uncertain outcomes.

Formulating ideas: Just as innovation master Michael Mauboussin draws lessons from science and psychology for investing, good innovators look for inspiration in nonobvious places. They seek *intersections*, situations in which people can bring fresh perspectives to old problems. Remember the guidance from the great artist Pablo Picasso: "Good artists copy, great artists steal."

Choosing between uncertain alternatives: Consider the CEO picking between several bold growth strategies, the twenty-eight-year-old consultant considering a career change, or the marketing manager debating whether to invest in Facebook, Twitter, or another emerging marketing channel. The complexity of choices can force many people to freeze or to get stuck in loops of endless analysis.[1] But you can't know for sure until you try. An external bias means that you actively experiment to see what works and what doesn't work. Instead of making decisions based on analysis of *ideas*, you make decisions based on analysis of *actions*.

---

1. If you want to blow your mind, read *Paradox of Choice: Why More Is Less*, by Barry Schwartz (New York: Ecco, 2004)—it describes how more choices actually leave us worse off.

Mike Tyson (Recognize That You Are Wrong)

I've seen too many innovators work tirelessly to develop the perfect plan. The end product of these efforts is often a thick binder that has good "thunk" value.[2] The binder has it all— industry analysis, financial forecast, profiles on current and would-be competitors, detailed roadmaps for next-generation products, illustrations, figures, embedded videos—and more!

The thinking that goes into those heavy stacks is valuable—it often leads to a more robust understanding of the industry that the innovator is targeting and what really is required for success. However, the last time I checked, banks don't accept "thunks" as legal currency.

One of history's most well-respected military strategists, Helmut von Moltke (the elder), was a Prussian general in the mid-nineteenth century.[3] The general believed in the value of detailed battle plans, but also said something that roughly translates to "no plan ever survived first contact with the battlefield." He knew that a military strategist had to be ready to change course once the battlefield revealed the weakness in his plan.

But instead of chiseling von Moltke on the Mount Rushmore of Innovation, I put the famous boxer Mike Tyson for his memorable line: "Everybody has a plan, until they get

---

2. Always good to have a bit of onomatopoeia in one's prose, even if *thunk* isn't a real word. I hope that its meaning is obvious—thunk value is something that makes a satisfying noise when dropped from a height of about eighteen inches onto a table. Consultants like to make sure their PowerPoint presentations have high thunk value.

3. *Wikipedia* tells us that von Moltke (the younger) was a German general who played a part in setting the stage for World War I.

punched in the face." Like it or not, if you are innovating, you *are* going to get punched in the face. No business plan survives first contact with the market. Innovators should start by assuming that their plans are partly right and partly wrong. The plan itself doesn't separate the winners from the losers. The reaction to adversity, the way in which you pivot (to use innovation master Steve Blank's language) is what separates the winners from the losers.

It's pretty liberating to recognize that there is no perfect plan. It also drives four strategic shifts:

1. Rethink the resources you throw behind an idea. It doesn't make sense to invest huge amounts of money behind an idea that probably has fatal flaws.

2. Change your planning approach. Once you recognize you are going to be wrong, it's easy to embrace what innovation master Rita McGrath calls a discovery-driven plan. The basics of discovery-driven planning are straightforward. As described earlier, you start by asserting your answer, then work backward to identify what needs to be true for that answer to be viable. Identify the critical assumptions, and then design and execute activities to learn more about those assumptions.

3. Develop a "portfolio" mind-set. No matter how much you might wish differently, there is a chance that your brilliant idea will turn out to be not so brilliant. So what's Plan B or Plan C? What else might you do to solve the problem facing you or your customer? If

you are a leader, what happens if two-thirds of the things your organization is working on don't pan out? Make sure you have a backup option.

4. Change how you measure innovators. Most companies assess performance on the basis of an individual's results. But if an innovative idea is by necessity flawed in some way, an innovator can do the right things and still fail. Leaders trying to ignite innovation have to move from rewarding innovation *outcomes* to rewarding *behaviors* consistent with successful innovation.

Thomas Edison (Release Your Inner Edison)

The conclusion to our 2008 book *The Innovator's Guide to Growth* included an homage to Thomas Edison.[4] While there is reasonable scholarly debate about the degree to which Edison deserved his sterling reputation, there is no doubt that the man could turn a phrase. Consider these Edison sound bites:

- "I never perfected an invention that I did not think about in terms of the service it might give others . . . I find out what the world needs, then I proceed to invent." Edison would have tipped his cap to A. G. Lafley's consumer-is-boss mind-set.

---

4. I am convinced that the best chapter in two of my three previous books was the conclusion. This is sad, because no one gets to the conclusion. I am trying consciously to break the trend in this book (though the conclusion is cool—I promise).

- "If I find 10,000 ways something won't work, I haven't failed. I am not discouraged, because every wrong attempt discarded is often a step forward." Punched in the face plenty of times, Edison kept plugging away.

- "Opportunity is missed by most people because it is dressed in overalls and looks like work."

- "Genius is 1 percent inspiration and 99 percent perspiration."

Releasing your inner Edison means living those last two quotes in particular. While this book's central thesis is that innovation is more approachable than ever before, that doesn't make innovation easy. Innovation is a discipline. And like any discipline, mastery comes through hours of hard work.

Of course, not everyone has an opportunity to have a transformational experience like working at a start-up, launching a game-changing product like Apple's iPad, or living in exotic locations. But think about how would-be marathoners train. They don't start by running twenty miles. Instead, they might go to the gym to begin conditioning their muscles for running. They then run a reasonably short distance and successively push out as their muscles get acclimated to longer distances.[5] You too can start modestly. Even changing your morning routine can begin to hardwire the skills

---

5. I'm at least told that this is the case. The last time I ran a mile was in seventh grade, when I was about six inches shorter and the same weight as I am now. It wasn't really running as much as it was, in its best light, walking briskly. I believe my time was about eighteen minutes. Roger Bannister I am not.

required to be a successful innovator. Of course, ideally you will expose yourself to greater and greater challenges, but you should always look for the relatively simple ways to practice.

Organizational leaders should consider what they can do to provide opportunities for their top talent to develop skills as innovators, because the way most organizations groom talent in fact systematically weeds out the innovators. In most companies, your reward for success is greater and greater responsibility. The more the organization looks to you to deliver on tomorrow's numbers, the less freedom you have to create new growth businesses. Organizations should consider intentionally giving their up-and-comers assignments that are more ambiguous so that these people develop the capabilities to deal with high degrees of uncertainty. That might actually mean giving them smaller assignments or moving them further from the core business to intentionally expose them to challenges that tone their innovation muscles.

Robert N. Anthony Sr.
(Fight the Sucking Sound of the Core)

Sitting above my desk at home is a 1983 *New York Times* syndicated cartoon called *Stockworth*, by Hinda Sterling and Herb Selesnick (figure 3-1). It features a conversation between two executives. The first man says, "Power is neither created nor destroyed. It is merely transferred," proudly noting how he is quoting ancient Chinese philosophy (and the law of conversation of energy). The other executive says,

FIGURE 3-1

Source: From *Stockworth: An American CEO* © 2011. Reprinted with permission from Sterling & Selesnick, Inc. (Beverly, MA).

"Net worth equals assets minus liabilities. Anthony, Essentials of Accounting."

Look up to my grandfather on the Mount Rushmore of Innovation to remember the notion of double-entry bookkeeping. Every transaction balances out. Every strength has a corresponding weakness.

The innovation masters have a variety of terms to describe this concept. Clayton Christensen guides people to analyze their organization's "resources, processes, and prioritization criteria." Vijay Govindarajan notes how all organizations have DNA that is impossible to notice but very powerful. Richard Foster talks about mental models that make it hard to see new opportunities. I call it the sucking sound of the core business.[6]

Regardless of the language used to describe it, you need to recognize that your core—business or personality—is a

6. I'm pretty sure this is an homage to how in 1992, presidential candidate Ross Perot said that signing the North American Free Trade Agreement would lead to a "giant sucking sound" of jobs moving from the United States to Mexico. But for the life of me, I can't remember when I first used the phrase. Nor can I remember if I actually borrowed it from an infinitely more eloquent colleague or client.

powerful magnet that can take the most powerful idea and turn it into something that has been done before.

To make it real, let's play the "Who Could Have?" game. The game involves picking a popular start-up, and asking what established company could have launched the start-up. Nine times out of 10 the established company actually had something in the works that didn't quite make it.

Consider Facebook. It wasn't preordained that Facebook was to be created by a student in his dorm room. When I ask audiences who could have created Facebook, they typically respond with technology companies like Microsoft, Google, Amazon, or Yahoo! These are valid answers. But I push the audience members by asking them why people use Facebook. One core reason is a simple way to share memories and images. What other company has historically helped people share memories and images? Kodak. Here's the interesting thing. The film giant had its fingers on Facebook as early as 2001. At the time, the company had purchased a company called Ofoto, one of the leading online album providers. How hard would it have been for Kodak to say, "You know, our tagline is 'Share memories, share lives.' Why don't we let people simply share album pictures? While we are at it, we can create a feature that allows people to share news items as well."

The idea was two steps away from Facebook. Of course, Kodak didn't take those steps. As James Joaquin, the cofounder of Ofoto, explained, "What Facebook did was people-centric, not photo-centric, and that was the huge shift."

Kodak succumbed to the sucking sound of the core, as did my team at *The Dartmouth* when we bungled our Internet strategy. It is a common and real problem that inhibits success with innovation. One leader from a company we advised put it nicely: "We're organized to deliver consistent, reliable results. And that's the problem."

Organizations seeking to break the sucking sound of the core need strong, active leadership. Successful organizations are hardwired to maintain and extend their success model; they have been trained to seek and stamp out things that appear to be deviations or distractions. Active leadership can provide protection from the "corporate antibodies" that seek out and destroy novel ideas. One thing leadership can do is to create a safe place for innovation. Imagine a quarantine that keeps the corporate antibodies from infecting new ideas. Leaders who develop what innovation master Roger Martin calls an "opposable mind" can combat the sucking sound of the core by adapting their leadership approach according to the circumstance.

If you ever find yourself stuck, look to the Mount Rushmore of Innovation to remember four critical innovation mindsets that enable successful innovation:

1. Be externally focused.
2. Recognize that your first idea is wrong.
3. Release your inner Edison, and start sweating.
4. Break the sucking sound of the core.

These mind-sets will form the underpinning of the twenty-eight-day innovation program. Before we get there, however, let's look at seven pitfalls standing in front of successful innovation.

CHAPTER 4

INNOVATION'S SEVEN DEADLY SINS

How to avoid the pitfalls standing in the way of success

Over the past few years, I've experimented with different ways to talk about the traps that litter the ground in front of the would-be innovator. Finally, during a speech in New Delhi in July 2010, something clicked. The seven deadly sins have very clear parallels in the world of innovation, serving as a useful and memorable way to highlight an innovator's most common mistakes. Four of these sins—pride, sloth, lust, and greed—can trip up all would-be innovators. Envy, wrath, and gluttony are particularly acute within large companies. Table 4-1 summarizes these sins and how to avoid them.

Pride and Overshooting

People love show-and-tell during presentations, so I usually carry a couple of props with me to illustrate key teaching points. One of my favorite props is a simple one that accompanies me on every trip—my razor. I hold up my razor and ask

TABLE 4-1

Innovation's seven deadly sins

Sin	What it is	How to avoid it
Pride	Forcing your view of quality onto the marketplace; often results in overshooting	Take an external viewpoint to make sure you understand how the customer measures quality.
Sloth	Having innovation efforts slow to a crawl	Release your inner Edison ("genius is 1 percent inspiration and 99 percent perspiration").
Gluttony	Suffering from the curse of abundance; leads to overly slow, overly linear innovation efforts	Embrace selective scarcity—constrain resources in the early stages of innovation to enable creativity.
Lust	Getting distracted by pursuing too many "bright, shiny objects"	Focus your innovation efforts; remember that destruction often precedes creation.
Envy	Creating an us-versus-them relationship between the core and new growth efforts	Actively celebrate both the core business and new growth efforts.
Wrath	Punishing risk takers severely	Reward behavior, not outcomes.
Greed	Impatience for growth; leads to prioritizing low-potential markets	Be patient for growth and impatient for results.

people what it is. Astute shavers in the audience will note that it is the Gillette Fusion ProGlide razor and razor blade system. It is a wonderful product. It has six blades—five on the face of the razor and a blade on the other side for trimming. This loyal customer thinks the ProGlide fulfills Gillette's brand promise of providing the "best a man can get."

I then tell people the hundred-plus-year history of The Gillette Company in ten seconds: "King Gillette started with a single-blade safety razor. Then Gillette introduced a double-edged blade. Then a razor with two blades. Then a razor with three blades. Then a razor with five blades. What do you think comes next?" I ask the audience.

I then show a chart that appeared in *The Economist* a few years ago (figure 4-1). The graph showed that if the technology followed a hyperbolic curve, we'd be looking at ten-plus blades in a few short years. I ask the audience members which of them is looking forward to their ten-blade razor. The question typically elicits a few chuckles. Of course, people would *take* a ten-blade razor. Would they pay premium prices for it? Most would not, as it would be too much performance for their needs. The innovation literature calls this *overshooting*. I call it the sin of *pride*—that is, trying to continue to make

FIGURE 4-1

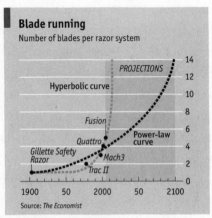

Source: Reprinted with permission of *The Economist*.

things better in your own mind even if it is not what the customer really wants or needs.

Fortunately, Gillette appears to be avoiding the sin of pride. The Fusion ProGlide was introduced in 2010. Instead of adding blades, Gillette made the blade more ergonomic and simpler to use. The improvements were based on deep research with customers to determine what frustrated them about shaving. That's the easiest way to avoid the sin of pride—make sure you are grounded in what the market wants, not what you want.

Sloth and Sweat

In the old fable "The Tortoise and the Hare," the slow and steady turtle ends up beating the fast-starting but arrogant hare in a race. While that occasionally happens in the innovation world, more often than not, innovation simply takes too long. By the time a company gets around to doing something, the window of opportunity has closed. Why does innovation take so long? It's not really laziness. It's that people work on the wrong activities, typically by prioritizing analysis over action.

It's easy to fill your day with activities that make it feel as if you are making progress tackling a problem. You can create a list of things to do and cross out some of the simple things on the list. You can create a detailed ninety-day plan that describes how you are going to achieve your objectives. You can research your idea. Or create a ninety-day plan for how you are going to do research. You might even create a spreadsheet that models the impact of the idea you are working on.

None of these things are bad. But remember, your first idea is almost always wrong. And you can't figure out precisely how it is wrong through analysis alone. You have to, you know, actually *do* something.

Remember innovation master Thomas Edison's teaching: if you're not sweating, you're not innovating.

Gluttony and the Curse of Abundance

Innovation master Richard Foster's first book carried the subtitle "The Attacker's Advantage." Foster described all the factors that give attackers a leg up over market leaders who have more to lose, who get stuck in their entrenched processes, and who find change scary and difficult. Foster is a very smart guy, and his analysis was absolutely right. But here's a challenging conundrum: one of the biggest problems an attacker must face is that the market leader usually has more resources than the attacker.

"Wait a second," you might be saying, "how can *more* resources be a problem?" It is the curse of abundance. Deep pockets allow companies to spend too many resources following the wrong strategy. They throw bodies against a problem, but everyone knows that small teams typically move faster than large teams. Companies are very patient for results, failing to realize that the patience actually hinders their ability to find innovation master Steve Blank's pivots.

I called my last book *The Silver Lining* because I believed that the constraints the economic shock of 2007–2008 placed on many companies would turn out to be good for innovation by forcing companies to do what they should have been doing already—embracing *selective scarcity* so that the luxury of abundance doesn't turn into a curse.

Lust and Bright, Shiny Objects

In 2007, we had Willy Shih sit in at a couple of Innosight's board meetings. Shih is a very sharp guy. Before joining the faculty of the Harvard Business School, he had an illustrious career at a range of operating companies, including IBM and Thomson. He had either the good fortune or the curse of running Kodak's digital operations in the late 1990s, which showed him firsthand how difficult it is for market leaders to respond to transformational change (in Kodak's case, digital imaging). In 2006, he joined the faculty at HBS as an adjunct professor to help Clayton Christensen teach his course. Shih quickly became a highly rated professor and a prolific writer of case studies.

During his first board meeting, Shih heard us describe our efforts to create a training offering, expand in Asia, step up our venture-capital activities, grow the revenues of our newsletter business, create a market research offering, open a merchant bank, and raise capital for a hedge fund.[1] At the time, we were a thirty-five-person company with about $8 million in global revenue.

Shih stopped the meeting and said, "You guys have a bright, shiny object problem." We were intellectually curious,

---

1. I will freely admit that I don't know what a merchant bank is, either.

which Shih said was good, but that led to us getting distracted by all the seemingly interesting things we *could* do. This meant we couldn't be world class at any of these things. As hard as it can be, innovators have to prioritize. In our case, it meant focusing on our core consulting business, investing in focused geographic expansion, finding a partner to push the training business, shifting and simplifying our publication strategy, and deprioritizing market research and venture capital and hedge fund activities, for the time being at least.

Never forget innovation master Joseph Schumpeter's idea of creative destruction. Stopping is as important as starting. Lust after too many things, and you'll find that you end up with nothing. Good innovators carefully choose the opportunities they go after, balancing breaking free from the sucking sound of the core with getting bogged down pursuing bright, shiny objects.

Envy and Sneetches with Stars

Most people would agree that the most famous graduate of Dartmouth College is a member of the Class of 1925 named Theodor Geisel. You might know him as Dr. Seuss, the author of notable literary works such as *The Cat in the Hat*, *Oh! The Places You'll Go*, and *The Sneetches and Other Stories.*

For those of you who don't remember the main story in that third book, there are two types of Sneetches, the "plain-bellied Sneetches" and the "Sneetches with stars upon thars." The Sneetches with stars generally consider themselves superior to the plain-bellied Sneetches. Then, one day, a man with an only-in-Seuss-land moniker of Sylvester McMonkey McBean arrives with a machine that can put a star on a Sneetch's belly.[2] The plain-bellied Sneetches eagerly get the procedure. Then, of course, the star isn't special anymore, so the man creates a star *removal* machine. Hilarity ensues. At the end of the story, the Sneetches have much less money but much more wisdom. The story has obvious lessons about the dangers of conformity and basing social status on silly, superficial things.

The parallel innovation sin occurs when innovators inside an organization proclaim themselves the chosen ones. They deride the core business and the backward mind-sets holding back growth. But remember, without that core business, there is no corporate innovation. And if a corporate innovator *isn't* using anything from the core, that person is picking a direct fight with entrepreneurs. Most of the time, the corporate innovators will lose that fight, decisively. While innovation master Vijay Govindarajan talks about forgetting, he talks about borrowing, too. His 2010 McKinsey Award–winning *Harvard Business Review* article (with co-author Chris Trimble) "Stop the Innovation Wars" urged companies to avoid internal sniping that can derail growth efforts. Leaders can guard against this problem by consistently celebrating both the core business efforts and the new-growth efforts.

There's a second, subtle Sneetches-with-stars problem that has less to do with envy but is still important. Companies

---

2. I debated for a good six minutes whether it was a Sneetch's belly or a Sneetches' belly, or even a Sneetches's belly. I don't think Strunk & White provides clear guidance on that one.

starting their innovation efforts often take their best perform-
ers, slap a star on their chests, and proclaim them innovators.
Sometimes that works. But often the people who are best in
the core business can struggle to adopt the new behaviors and
mind-sets required for successful innovation. Companies need
to think about staffing innovation efforts in different ways,
with people who have more developed innovation skills.

Wrath and Big Sticks

Corporate leaders frequently ask something along the lines
of "What incentives will motivate my people to be more
innovative?" Behind that question often lies a lurking fear
that companies—particularly big, publicly traded companies—are hamstrung because they can't possibly match the
upside that is available to entrepreneurs who start their own
companies.

Daniel Pink's wonderful book *Drive* shows how providing financial rewards for creatively oriented tasks actually
decreases performance. Instead, Pink suggests that good performance comes from providing autonomy, opportunities to
obtain mastery, and a sense of purpose to activities. Beyond
what they reward (the carrot), leaders also need to think
carefully about what they punish (the stick). A wrathful
leader punishes innovation failures, using lines such as "Failure
is not an option." But in innovation failure is most certainly
an option. Beautiful business plans don't always turn into
beautiful businesses. Remember, you need to pay at least as
much attention to the behaviors people follow as to the

results they achieve. Many venture-capital investors look to invest in entrepreneurs who have a couple failed ventures on their résumé—as long as those entrepreneurs learned lessons from those failures.

Big companies often severely punish people who work on failed ventures. What kind of message does it send if you punish people who take well-thought-out risks that don't pan out? Do you think it motivates people to take any kind of risk at all?

If you want to encourage innovation, think about what gets rewarded and what gets punished. Both are important.

Greed and Impatience for Growth

Michael Douglas's character Gordan Gekko told the world in the movie *Wall Street*, "Greed, for lack of a better word, is good." Legions of corporate titans follow that mantra, believing that the pursuit of profits leads to efficient markets and substantial consumer benefits.

Greed has its advantage, but innovators need to make sure they are greedy for the right thing. Often, innovators get greedy for growth. They want something that is as big as possible. Why could that possibly be a problem? If you look for quick growth, you are forced to look to what exists. After all, it is hard to make the case that a market that doesn't exist will be huge. But innovation master Clayton Christensen's research shows how hard it is for outsiders to realize booming growth in existing markets, because the incumbents in those markets have a lot to lose and will fight fiercely for every dollar of revenue.

The best innovators avoid the temptation to go after large, obvious, immediate markets. These people can be patient for growth. They should absolutely be greedy for results that demonstrate that the approach they are following has merits.

While chapters 1 through 3 described innovation and the tools and mind-sets needed to foster it, this chapter summarized how to fight the seven deadly sins of innovation that can pull you off course.

Now you are now ready to use these tools and the understanding you have gained to embark on a systematic program to grow innovation in your company. Part 2, "The 28-Day Innovation Program," will help you do just that.

PART TWO

THE 28-DAY INNOVATION PROGRAM

The rest of *The Little Black Book of Innovation* describes a twenty-eight-day innovation program. Each day provides an action-oriented tip to get better at innovation. There are four weeks in the program:

- Week 1: Discovering Opportunities

- Week 2: Blueprinting Ideas

- Week 3: Assessing and Testing Ideas

- Week 4: Moving Forward

Each day of training starts with the central question the day's training addresses and a brief answer to the question. I then describe the answer in greater detail, illustrating key points with case studies. Each day contains how-to tips to put the day's central idea into action immediately. As mentioned in the introduction, this program can be done in order, or it can be done episodically. Some of the suggested activities could take more than a single day. But immediate practice will help you build a strong foundation for more in-depth innovation efforts.

WEEK 1

DISCOVERING OPPORTUNITIES

While innovation can appear to be random, the best innovators follow a disciplined process to discover opportunities to do something different that has impact. The first week of innovation training focuses on this discovery process, drawing on experiences ranging from Innosight's efforts to help an Indian conglomerate reframe the local refrigerator market to surprising lessons from Looney Tunes.

The best way to practice these techniques is to apply them to a real problem. You might already have an innovative idea you hope to implement. If not, consider a problem at work or at home that has been nagging you. This week will help you to accomplish the following:

1. Identify your target customer.

2. Identify the problem the customer is struggling to solve today.

3. Discover any signals suggesting that the customer is dissatisfied with the status quo.

Day 1
Start Before You Need To

Central Question	One-Sentence Answer
How do I know it is time to innovate?	Watch for early warning signs, because the urgency of innovation and the ability to innovate are inversely related.

If you've started the twenty-eight-day innovation program, the odds are pretty high that you recognize the importance of innovation. But still, you might be thinking, "Do I really need to go through all of this? Innovation seems hard. How can I tell if I truly need to innovate?"

It's a reasonable question. My answer begins in a nonobvious place. Pause for a minute to think about the wonderful efficiency of the modern post office. Seems crazy, right? But this is a business that in most countries visits every single address at least five days a week, if not more. While everyone has stories of losing something in the mail, the overwhelming majority of mail comes on time and unharmed. It really is quite miraculous.

Of course, in a digital era, it also feels dangerously antiquated. The rise of modern technologies has placed severe pressure on the post office. Here's the problem, however. Exactly when was it clear that the U.S. Post Office was in trouble?

One natural point would be in 1994, when Netscape introduced its browser, marking the beginning of the modern Internet era. That's fine, but the volume of mail didn't slow down as e-mail and other forms of instant connections increased their penetration. In fact, along some dimensions, the rise of the commercial Internet increased demand for traditional mail service. After all, e-commerce of physical products requires delivery (in 2010, DVD rental provider Netflix reported shipping two million DVDs *a day* through the U.S. Postal Service!). And new technologies allowed companies to fine-tune their direct-mail marketing campaigns, making these efforts more economical.[1]

So perhaps it wasn't clear that the U.S. Postal Service had to change until about 2007, when the volume of mail actually started to decline. Here's the problem—by the time it was clear to everyone that the post office had to change, change was much more difficult. I call this the *innovator's paradox*. When times are good, you have the ability to do things differently, but not much urgency or desire. When times are bad, you urgently need to do things differently, but it's punishingly hard. Why? Companies end up spending most of their time dealing with what appears to be a sudden crisis in their core business. The cash flow that would support new

---

1. You know why you get so much junk mail? Because it works. As long as about one in a hundred customers takes action, direct mail is a very cost-effective form of marketing.

efforts has dried up. New-growth efforts look too small to address today's problems. The company needs to do something dramatic, but dramatic efforts rarely work. Innovation master Clayton Christensen calls this the "growth gap death spiral," meaning the efforts that companies take to plug growth gaps actually result in larger, not smaller, gaps.

This pattern, punishingly, repeats itself in industry after industry. In the summer of 2006, I was doing a workshop for senior leaders in a large media company. I was talking about potentially significant changes in the industry and brought up YouTube, then a fledgling service mostly populated by pirated videos.

An audience member challenged me. "If you add up every video ever watched on YouTube, it is less than the viewership of even low-rated television shows on obscure cable networks," he said. "We don't have to worry about this garbage."

Of course, the audience member was correct at the time, but YouTube's rapid growth—further powered by Google's acquisition of the company in 2006—has transformed YouTube into a powerful force in the television industry. And in 2010, Google itself began inching into the television market.

Kodak president Philip Faraci compellingly described the innovator's paradox during a panel discussion I moderated at a newspaper industry convention in 2008.[2] Of course,

---

2. Clearly, the newspaper industry suffered from the innovator's paradox as well. Despite all the stories about the industry's demise in the late 1990s, the industry looked stronger and more profitable in the early 2000s than before the commercialization of the Internet. Of course, lurking underneath the surface were powerful forces that would lead to dramatic change—most of it for the negative.

Kodak was well aware of the transformational potential of digital imaging. But, in Faraci's words, "the core business just kept growing." In 1999, its photography business peaked at $10.3 billion. The business looked stable in 2000, with sales a robust $10.2 billion. Sure, it shrank 8 percent in 2001 to $9.4 billion, but that was in the midst of a tough recession. Declines accelerated from there (revenues dropped to less than $1 billion by the end of the decade), but it was legitimately hard for Kodak leadership to square the story they kept hearing ("the future is digital!") with the data ("the future is still in the future").

It's just hard to believe there's a crisis when the data isn't conclusive. And, as noted in one of my favorite lines, which is buried in the conclusion of *Seeing What's Next*, "by the time the writing is on the wall, everyone can read it."[3]

Every family has a variant of this story—the free-spending uncle who suddenly lost his job and got swamped by debt; the cousin whose chronic choice of work over family life led to divorce; the coworker whose bad eating and exercise habits led to a debilitating heart attack. Again, the pattern is the same. Everything looks OK, until the day when it doesn't. And when that day comes, the degrees of freedom to do things differently have markedly decreased.

---

3. Yet another example of saving the best for last. I wonder how many people actually read the conclusion of Clayton M. Christensen, Scott D. Anthony, and Erik A. Roth, *Seeing What's Next*? I swear, it's pretty good.

So, what do you do? If you want to understand the need for change, don't just look at where things stand today. Instead, ask three questions:

1. What do the underlying trends suggest could be possible future states? In the post office's case, the slowing rate of growth compared with historical norms could have been enough of a warning sign that serious change was necessary. We actually helped the media company mentioned above to do some straightforward scenario analysis to show what would happen if it ended up in a "perfect storm" of change. The results were scary enough—and some of the responses simple enough—that it motivated serious action. Clearly, financial planners and doctors play similar roles, showing—in sometimes very sophisticated ways—the impact of following a particular behavior.

2. Where is there a small but growing trend? When he reviewed a draft of this book, innovation thought leader Karl Ronn (who will be pivotal in later Day 6) offered this thought: "Anything that has doubled its size is a potential disruptor, regardless of size. They are running the test market we should have run. This is a simple way to not ignore small stuff." Like most of Ronn's suggestions, it is a good one.

3. What can you learn from analogies and metaphors? Kodak, the post office, and the media company faced a common threat—replacement by "good enough,"

cheaper alternatives. They aren't the only three organizations that faced this type of change. Christensen's *Innovator's Dilemma* provides similar examples from industries as wide ranging as hard disk drive manufacturers, excavators, and accounting software. It is always worth asking whether you see something that looks similar to a situation faced by a successful organization in its past.

You often need a keen eye and some creativity to spot signals of change before they are abundantly clear. It's worth expending the effort, however, when the alternative is getting stuck in a death spiral or a paradox.

HOW-TO TIPS

✓ Go to a popular financial Web site, and determine whether your current savings rate and your desired future lifestyle intersect.

✓ Create a list of three signposts that would suggest that you or your company need to dramatically shift strategy.

✓ Look at the ten highest-performing stocks for the last twelve months. Discuss with a friend whether any of them show signs of being stuck in the innovator's paradox.

Day 2
Remember, the Consumer Is Boss

Central Question	One-Sentence Answer
How do I spot opportunities for innovation?	Take a consumer-is-boss perspective.

On March 7, 2000, Procter & Gamble warned that it would miss its quarterly earnings estimates. This event might not seem like that big a deal—after all, companies miss their earnings estimates all the time. But not *P&G*. The company had only missed its estimates once since World War II. The March 2000 announcement sent its stock price down a shocking 31 percent. Three months later, P&G chairman and CEO Durk Jager stepped down, and P&G's board appointed innovation master A. G. Lafley to the role of CEO (he became chairman in 2002). P&G's stock dropped another 11 percent that week.

As Lafley started the hard work of reinvigorating P&G, he made a critical decision to focus on winning through innovation—one that ultimately helped him earn a spot on the Mount Rushmore of Innovation. The decision resulted from Lafley's core belief that innovation was a discipline that could be managed and mastered. He set about weaving innovation deeply through P&G's culture.

As part of this effort, Lafley sought to get P&G employees to shift their focus. The company was world renowned for

Courtesy of P&G

A.G. Lafley

driving decisions based on deep customer understanding, but upon reflection, Lafley realized that the company had drifted away from that understanding.

"We were all so busy every day," Lafley told me. "We had our ears in our cell phones; we had our heads in our Black-Berries and PDAs; we had our heads in our computer screens; we were consumed in meetings of all kinds. When you thought about it, where was our behind? Our face was internal, and our behind was right facing the customer."

Lafley is gifted at communicating complicated ideas in simple ways. He developed a simple mantra to refocus P&G: The consumer is boss. He would say something along these lines: "Fellow P&G-ers, I'd like you to meet your new boss. You may think that I, as your CEO, am boss. That's not right. You might think that the Board of Directors to which I report is boss. That's not right. You might think our shareholders are the bosses. That's not right. You might think your line manager is boss. That's not right. We have one and only one boss that matters. The consumer. The consumer is boss."

Lafley urged P&G to listen to the consumer as the company never had before. P&G had to hear what the consumer was saying and, much more importantly, tease out what the consumer couldn't articulate.

Lafley urged particular focus on the two "moments of truth"—the moment a consumer chooses a product, and the moment the consumer uses a product. P&G had to learn more about these moments of truth—where it was falling short, and where there were opportunities for innovation.

"The consumer is boss" wasn't just an executive platitude. P&G increased investment in market research. It sought to get employees out of the building to spend time with consumers. It launched two programs, Living It and Working It. The basic notion is that everyone in P&G—from the chairman down—would spend time living with consumers, shopping with consumers, or working alongside consumers. Many products trace their inspiration to these kinds of efforts. For example, watching a woman grow frustrated when she spilled coffee grounds on her floor helped to inspire P&G's Swiffer quick cleaning line.

If you happen to meet a P&G employee, ask him or her about a recent consumer contact. Odds are, the employee's face will light up as the person describes what he or she has learned from spending time with a consumer. The company's offices are blanketed with pictures of consumers. Marketing plans are littered with pictures and icons to bring consumers to life.

Other companies follow derivations of the consumer-is-boss mind-set. Best Buy doesn't rely on dry customer-segmentation models. Rather, it gives names and personalities to segment archetypes to help bring them to life. I even once heard a story—perhaps apocryphal, given that no names were mentioned—of a company that brought a mannequin into a key decision meeting to help make sure the consumer had a seat at the table.

The consumer-is-boss mind-set is useful whether or not you actually serve end consumers. After all, just about everyone has a "customer." A salesperson has a sales contact. A member of the IT support team serves the company's employees. And many companies have more than one "boss" that they must please. P&G's most important customers aren't individuals—they are Walmart, Carrefour, Target, and the millions of mom-and-pop retailers around the world. If P&G doesn't figure out what will delight those retailers, it will have no hope of delighting the end consumer. Medical-device companies have to think about the doctors and nurses who use their products, insurance companies that pay for medical procedures, hospitals that purchase the product, government regulators, patients, and those patients' families.

A consumer-is-boss mind-set trains you to look at the world through other people's eyes. It helps you feel their hopes, dreams, frustrations, and desires. And that understanding provides absolutely critical input to spot opportunities for innovation, which, after all, is the goal of this week's exercises.

Taking this mind-set can also help you defuse disputes at home and at work. It's simple, but the empathy that comes from taking a different perspective can help you see things you might otherwise have missed.

For example, a couple of years ago, I was frustrated by upward feedback I received from one of our junior consultants.

I spoke with my colleague Dave Duncan about my frustration. "This feedback is just empirically wrong," I said. "I just don't know how he could have this perspective."

"You know," Duncan said, "I received feedback that I felt the same way about in the last review cycle. At first I ranted about it, because the feedback literally bordered on lunacy. However, the person who gave it believed it fiercely. So I asked myself what I had done that led to a smart individual's having such a warped perspective."

I now try to always follow Duncan's advice. After all, our perspectives are always right in our own mind. Step out of yourself and ask questions like "What assumptions was that person making when he or she made that statement? What else in this person's life might have influenced what was said?"

After all, the consumer is boss.

HOW-TO TIPS

- ✓ Bring your target customers to life—give them a name, describe what they do, and find images you associate with them.

- ✓ Detail the amount of time you spent with customers or key stakeholders in the last three months. Find a way to triple that time.

- ✓ Look back at a recent disagreement you had at work or at home—use a consumer-is-boss mind-set to try to identify what was behind your antagonist's argument.

Day 3
Get the Job Done

Central Question	One-Sentence Answer
What indicates an opportunity for innovation?	Look for an important, unsatisfied job to be done, or a problem the customer can't adequately address today.

One of the biggest challenges facing the would-be innovator is developing an understanding of the unsatisfied wants, needs, and desires that indicate opportunities for innovative approaches.

I can tell you how *not* to do this. Don't go to a current or prospective customer and ask, "What do you want?" Most customers actually don't do a very good job answering that question. And too frequently, that starting point leads to a more pleading, "Why won't you buy more of what I am trying to sell?"

At Innosight, we use language popularized by innovation master Clayton Christensen. In *The Innovator's Solution*, Christensen and co-author Michael Raynor described the notion of a "job to be done." The concept is very simple. People don't *buy* products and services; people *hire* them to get jobs done.

In his speeches, Christensen illustrates the example with a humorous story about a fast-food company trying to accelerate the sales of milkshake products. While the company thinks that the competition is milkshakes sold by other fast-food competitors, deeper investigation highlights two different jobs to be done. In the morning, drivers facing the prospect of a long, boring commute are looking for a "commuting companion." They appreciate the milkshake's viscosity (it takes twenty minutes to consume the milkshake!), the drink's ability to be consumed one-handed, and its ability to provide caloric coverage for the morning. In the afternoon, parents who have been saying no to their kids all day are looking for a "simple placation tool." The rub, Christensen notes, is that the features that delight the morning commuter infuriate the parent, who wants something less viscous and smaller.

Christensen's language channels thoughts of other great management leaders. As described earlier in the book, innovation master Peter Drucker detailed a similar idea a half-century ago: "The customer rarely buys what the company thinks it sells him. One reason for this is, of course, that nobody pays for a 'product.' What is paid for is satisfaction." Companies think they are selling products or services, but the customer doesn't think of the world that way. Customers have problems, and the company has potential solutions. Harvard Business School guru Ted Levitt, who authored four award-winning *Harvard Business Review* articles, including my personal favorite, "Marketing Myopia," allegedly told his students, "People don't want quarter-inch drills—they want quarter-inch holes."[4]

The simple question of "What job is the customer struggling to get done?" is a very powerful way to identify opportunities for innovation.

Here's an example of how this question helped refine Innosight's service offering. At its core, Innosight is a strategy consulting company. This means that we get hired to help solve a problem that a company doesn't think it can solve on its own. Our specialty is innovation, so typically clients will ask us about creating work processes to support innovation, coaching executives to make them more innovation friendly, helping them identify opportunities, and so on.

During a strategic review in 2010, we reflected on a project we did a few years earlier with a major beverage company. The client had asked us to identify new growth opportunities. We thought it was a great project. We developed compelling, creative ideas. Our final meeting ended in a standing ovation. One of the ideas we highlighted ended up being the basis for a billion-dollar brand.

Was the project a success? We did what the client asked us to do. We earned a standing ovation. However, our client didn't do anything with our insight. A different company launched that billion-dollar brand.

So, we asked, *why* did the client ask us to identify new growth opportunities? Our task wasn't to earn a standing

---

4. This quote has appeared in a range of Innosight-authored books, but no one has ever found documented proof that Levitt actually said this. He did write "Marketing Myopia," which appeared in *Harvard Business Review* in 1960, however, and it is amazing how fifty years after the article's publication, it still rings powerfully and painfully true for many readers.

ovation, conduct analysis, or put together a beautiful Power-Point presentation. The client's real job to be done was to achieve growth that was otherwise out of its reach. By that measure, the project was a failure.

This insight helped us realize that in some circumstances, words, guidance, and advice were insufficient. Sometimes clients needed someone who could help breathe life into new-growth businesses. We decided to form a team of specialists under the name "Innosight Labs" to help get this job done.[5]

The job-to-be-done lens is critical for any challenge that requires innovation. For example, if you work for an IT department, ask what job the end user is really trying to get done (in many cases, it is to not think about IT at all). If you are trying to sort out a difficult relationship with a coworker, ask what job he or she is really trying to get done.

Now, of course, if you go to your customers and ask them what job they are trying to get done, you are likely to be met with a blank stare. One of the easiest things to do is to just keep asking "Why?" until you start to get to that fundamental problem. For example:

- Why did you buy a drill? *I needed to drill a hole.*

- Why did you need to drill a hole? *I needed to hang a picture.*

---

5. The series of insights that helped lead to this decision also provided a good way to conceptualize how to overcome the barriers that stand between good business plans and good businesses. This will be the subject of my next book, tentatively titled *Paving the First Mile: Bridging the Gap Between Beautiful Plans and Beautiful Businesses*, due to come out in 2013. My colleague Matt Eyring will be coauthoring this one with me.

- Why did you need to hang a picture? *I wanted to make the living room look nicer.*

- Why did you want to make the room look nicer? *My mother-in-law made an offhand comment about the room last time she was here, and I don't want that to happen again.*

And so on. Careful analysis goes beyond functional consideration to get at emotional (how someone feels about himself or herself) and social (how someone relates to others) areas as well. The goal is to move from the solution to the problem, because deep understanding of the problem can make the solution obvious.

Simple questions can lead to powerful insight. Whenever you are looking for opportunities for innovation, remember to ask, "What job is the customer struggling to get done?"

HOW-TO TIPS

- ✓ Keep asking "Why?" to determine the job your current offering or innovative idea gets done.

- ✓ Keep a diary for twenty-four hours, noting the points of frustration you encounter throughout the day, to train yourself to spot signs of frustration.

- ✓ Get out of the building (you'll be doing this again later this week). Watch a prospective customer go about his or her day. Write down three jobs this person is struggling to get done.

Day 4
Compete Against Nonconsumption

Central Question	One-Sentence Answer
Which customers should I target?	Look for "nonconsumers" that face a barrier inhibiting their ability to get a job done.

Back in 2006, an Indian conglomerate called Godrej & Boyce came to us with a question: "How can we break out of our refrigerator death match against General Electric, Whirlpool, and LG?" For years, the company had been fighting fiercely against global powerhouses with trusted brands for the very small portion of the Indian market that purchased a standard Western refrigerator.

We flipped the problem on its head. Instead of competing against the powerhouses for the 15 percent of the market that purchased refrigerators, what about the 85 percent that did *not* purchase refrigerators?

We were following guidance—guidance worded in different ways—from innovation gurus Clayton Christensen ("compete against nonconsumption"), W. Chan Kim, and Renée Mauborgne ("find blue oceans unpopulated by powerful competitors"), and C. K. Prahalad ("target the fortune

Photo by Soumik Kar

at the bottom of the economic pyramid"). Whatever name you want to give it, if you are trying to discover an opportunity for innovation, one time-tested innovation trick is to look for people who face some kind of constraint that inhibits their ability to solve a pressing problem they are facing in their lives. Specifically, look for people who find existing solutions too complicated, expensive, or difficult to access.

Why did 85 percent of the Indian market not buy refrigerators? It's not rocket science. Refrigerators are relatively expensive. Many Indians considered them unaffordable luxuries. Even if Indians could afford the refrigerator itself, the expensive electricity required to run the power-hungry appliance made the total cost of ownership high. Unreliable electricity rendered plug-based refrigerators worthless. Finally, for the many Indians who lived in small shacks in crowded slums, a refrigerator was simply too big for their dwelling.

It's not that these consumers didn't want some of the benefits of refrigeration. But it was out of their reach. The question for Godrej now was, what would delight these customers? What were some of the jobs they were trying to get done?

Godrej went out and spent time with customers to learn that it could address two important jobs. Many of the male workers in the household spent fourteen or more hours a day doing back-breaking labor in intense heat. "I wish I could give myself a simple reward. Just a cold drink at the end of a long day," a laborer might say. The laborer's wife had a different job to be done. "I'm tired of spending my entire life preparing food. Couldn't I just store food for one extra day?" she might ask. Note how different these jobs are from a Westerner, who organizes meals in advance, visits supermarkets once a week, and so on.

With this insight, Godrej designed a very different kind of refrigerator. In 2009, the firm introduced a product called ChotuKool. The first version looked like a small cooler. It was battery powered and had a chiller that functioned a bit like a fan that cools a laptop's battery. It was top loading, so power wouldn't dissipate when the door was opened. The top of the refrigerator actually resembled a smile. And, most importantly, it cost about $70, sharply cheaper than comparable products. The product exceeded sales expectations during a trial launch in 2010. In early 2011, Godrej won an award from the Indian prime minister for its efforts, with sales accelerating dramatically.

This kind of "nonconsumption" existed in the Anthony living room as well. From 1978 to 2003, I was the quintessential consumer of video gaming technology. I had every video game system known to man. The first one I remember is the Atari 2600 and the classic game *Star Raiders* (my parents tell me we had a TRS-80, but I don't recall playing on that). Then there was the ColecoVision, the Nintendo, the Sega Genesis, the Super Nintendo, the TurboGraphx 16, the Sega Dreamcast, the PlayStation, and the PlayStation 2. Then, in 2003, it stopped. The video game system went in the closet. What do you think happened in my life in 2003?

If you are anything like audiences during my talks, about half of you think I had a baby in 2003. Actually, our first child came in 2005. In 2003, I got married. That—and working to get Innosight's consulting arm off the ground—was enough complexity in my life to kill the complicated video game system. You see, Sony and Microsoft had gotten caught in a death struggle for the most demanding video game customer—fast-fingered teenage boys who must have the most realistic game play and the most intense graphics. Chasing that target led to video games that were so complicated, so difficult to use, that it would take three weeks to figure out how to play them. And I just didn't have that kind of time anymore.

So I, along with many, many other nongamers, eagerly awaited Nintendo's Wii system. The magic of the Wii wasn't the console's beautiful graphics. It was the controller. The controller contained a chip called an accelerometer, which tracked motion along multiple dimensions. You picked the controller up and interfaced with the system in ways that were previously unimaginable. It was so simple, so intuitive, that by the time he was three, my son Charlie was an accomplished baseball player on the Wii. He could never mash buttons or master multiple joysticks, but he sure knew how to swing a clublike instrument.

Nintendo's strategy was very conscious. It was trying to grow the market by appealing to people who were put off by the complexity of other systems. And the strategy was a massive success. Over the subsequent five years, the Wii outsold the competition by a substantial margin and, in so doing, created billions of dollars of profits for Nintendo. The company basically had the casual gaming market to itself for five years until Microsoft and Sony finally introduced competitive products in late 2010.

The great thing about this kind of strategy is that the target customer can be satisfied with something simple or straightforward, because, after all, something is better than nothing!

I've seen this concept applied inside organizations, too. The last thing many people want to do is call up human resources to ask a question about their benefits or spend hours with the IT department to figure out how to install new software on their computer. Think about how you can give people the tools to solve problems on their own.

It takes some mental discipline to look to markets that don't exist, but the discipline can pay off in the form of exciting growth opportunities that are hidden in plain sight.

HOW-TO TIPS

✓ Identify two things that you use every day and that competed against nonconsumption.

✓ Write down five things that a coworker or friend can only do by relying on an expert or going to a central location. Think about ideas that would let these people do it themselves.

Day 5
Find Compensating Behaviors

Central Question	One-Sentence Answer
How can I find nonobvious opportunities?	Consider targeting the compensating behavior that an individual follows to cover the inadequacy of existing solutions.

In 2009, we were consulting to VF Corporation's Jeanswear division, which sells popular brands such as Wrangler and Lee. The company told us that its goal was to become the "Procter & Gamble of the apparel world." What did that mean? Most apparel companies are fashion or trend driven. They hire cutting-edge designers who in essence seek to always be one step ahead of customers. VF wanted to be market driven. It wanted to understand the customer better than any of their competitors and use that insight to drive the creation of innovative solutions.

With this in mind, we guided the company to spend more time with current and prospective customers to find points of frustration. One trip to a local department store proved particularly illuminating. Executives watched as a prospective female customer shopped for a new pair of jeans. She wandered around the endless racks of clothes in the store, picking up pair of jeans after pair of jeans. She staggered under the weight of the jeans as she entered the dressing room.

As the team reflected on its observation, it highlighted two peculiarities. First, the sheer volume of jeans the woman brought into the dressing room seemed surprising. Second, the woman had picked up multiple sizes of just about every pair she was trying on.

Then came the most important part of the visit—trying to understand what was behind the woman's behavior. The executives assumed that she must have recently experienced a weight change, so she was unsure of her size. Actually, it turned out that her experience taught her that the sizes that appeared on the labels of jeans only loosely related to what would actually fit. She had to bring in seemingly dozens of pairs of jeans to find one good fit. Even worse, after a couple of washes, the jeans wouldn't fit quite the same, leaving the woman highly frustrated.

Illustrated by Alexander Rothman

Now, along some dimensions, this doesn't exactly qualify as a blinding insight (especially to women). Research shows that women find shopping for jeans to be the second-most intimidating shopping experience, behind shopping for swimwear. But the experience helped the apparel company understand what customers did to work around the limitation of current products. And these were the customers who had chosen to come to the retail store—just think of the legions of customers who found the process so depressing that they wouldn't even step foot in the store! These observations helped the company focus its innovation efforts on the jeans-buying process. VF changed the labeling on its jeans, developed innovative display mechanisms in retail stores, and launched an online campaign where noted style icon Stacey London helped women find jeans that would be most appropriate for their body type. In early 2011, VF Corporation reported that these and related innovation efforts had created $100 million in incremental revenue in its Jeanswear division.

Innovation master A. G. Lafley found a similar workaround when he was a young brand manager at Procter & Gamble working on Tide laundry detergent. P&G would regularly administer quantitative surveys to assess the quality of its product and packaging. Consumers frequently reported that they loved Tide's packaging (at the time, Tide was packaged in cardboard boxes). Yet, when Lafley was interacting with a consumer, he noticed that she almost always used a screwdriver or scissors to open the Tide box. Lafley realized that the woman didn't want to risk breaking her nails opening the cardboard box. She said she loved the packaging because she didn't know of any alternatives, but in reality, she had to find a creative way to open the box because of its design limitations.

Careful observation can help to highlight these kinds of *compensating behaviors*, or ways people work around the limitations of existing solutions. Drilling into these compensating behaviors can help to unearth innovation opportunities. It is yet another reminder of how important it is to look at the world through the customer's eyes when you are searching for opportunities.

Sometimes, a customer-first perspective highlights nonobvious opportunities; other times, it highlights nonobvious competitive threats. Consider a conversation I had with a colleague in India. One thing you can count on in India is that the length of a car trip is impossible to predict. A drive that is five minutes one day can be fifty the next. Weather plays a role, as does the migration pattern of animals, local politics, and what appears to be sheer randomness.

"Here's a provocative perspective," my colleague said in late 2009, when our "fifteen-minute drive" entered its second hour. "I think the Tata Nano is going to be a disappointment."

I gulped. We had been heralding the transformational perspective of the Nano for some time. The story featured prominently in my colleague Mark Johnson's then forthcoming book *Seizing the White Space*. It is a legitimately great story. Indian legend Ratan Tata—the head of the Tata Group of companies that touched every sector of the Indian economy and had total revenues of more than $70 billion—had the idea when watching a family of four struggling to traverse crowded Indian streets on a tiny scooter. He challenged his team with developing the "people's car," something that would sell for an unheard-of low price of one *lakh*, or roughly $2,500. He hoped people would trade in their unsafe scooters for much safer Nanos.

The team delivered on Ratan Tata's promise. It followed innovative approaches to develop the Nano, like outsourcing close to 90 percent of the Nano's parts and considering out-of-the-box options like semi-finished kits that rural entrepreneurs could assemble into fully finished cars. Tata had to make trade-offs as well; the most basic Nano model lacked working air-conditioning or power windows.

So why was my colleague skeptical?

"Look at it from the customer's perspective," he said. "These people could already afford to pay twenty-five hundred dollars for a perfectly good used car. Instead, they consciously chose the scooter."

Why would consumers choose a scooter? It wasn't that these people didn't care about their family. Rather, they didn't have the space to park a car, or they found scooters that fit into the tiny gaps on India's chaotic streets a much more convenient form of transportation.

Indeed, early Nano sales disappointed (early production problems and bad publicity played a role, too). Further, initial customers tended not to be people who were replacing scooters; rather, the stylish car appealed to the up-and-coming middle class, which used the car to make a statement to friends and family. If the Nano continued to follow that path, it might be a commercial success, but it would fail to achieve Ratan Tata's inspirational vision.

Remember, our goal in week 1 is to discover a high-potential innovation opportunity. Look at the world through the eyes of the target customers. Find out how they are getting the job done. If it is a messy workaround, you may have found a great opportunity. If they are perfectly satisfied with their solution, look somewhere else.

HOW-TO TIPS

✓ Lead a round-table discussion to identify compensating behaviors that your company's solution forces customers to follow.

✓ Identify one compensating behavior you follow between the hours of 7 a.m. and noon. Discuss this with a friend or colleague.

Day 6
Get as Close to Context as Possible

Central Question	One-Sentence Answer
How should I investigate potential opportunities?	Start with deep observational or ethnographic research; avoid focus groups like the plague.

Discovering jobs to be done and compensating behaviors can seem daunting. Many people assume this kind of discovery requires heavy-duty statistical analysis of large-sample quantitative surveys. That kind of research has its place. But it is just as important to be like an anthropologist who carefully observes indigenous peoples to determine their unstated needs and wants or to figure out the behaviors they are following but can't quite articulate.

Perhaps the best example of insight through observation is Sony's legendary Akio Morita, the man behind the Walkman, the portable compact disc player, and a range of other market-creating innovations. Morita was famous for avoiding quantitative market research. Instead, his research involved him and a small group of colleagues going out to just . . . watch . . . what people did, or didn't do.

One of my good friends is Karl Ronn, who during the first decade of the 2000s was one of the leading innovators inside Procter & Gamble (he left P&G in 2010). Ronn is one of those rare people who can flip from explaining how P&G's products work at a molecular level (he has a degree in chemical engineering) to describing the look in a mother's eyes the first time she experienced the easy cleaning of Swiffer, one of the megabrands that Ronn helped to introduce.[6] One of Ronn's pet peeves about innovation is how much people rely on information gleaned from small-group discussions with prospective customers—the ubiquitous focus group. His verbal rant on the topic was so powerful that I asked him to write down his perspective. He wrote:

> If I had one thing to change in consumer research, it would be to ban focus groups, especially the ones that you don't lead yourself. Focus groups are left over from an earlier era. Focus groups are for lazy people. Not lazy consumers—lazy researchers. Go to where the person is doing the task, and watch them do it and then do it with them. You have no conscious memory of how you do routine tasks. So, when you bring consumers together in a focus group room and ask them

---

6. Remember the old adage, "Success has many siblings but failure is an orphan"? I've met literally hundreds of people inside P&G who claim to have worked on the Swiffer, and dozens of design companies and research agencies. For the record, I had absolutely nothing to do with the Swiffer, though we were early adopters in 1999, as my wife (then girlfriend) found that it was the only way to get me involved in cleaning our Cambridge apartment.

Karl Ronn

two hours of questions about something they can't remember, how many new insights can you get? Take the same two hours, and visit four people at home or at a bar or in a store, and suddenly they are in an environment where they can show you exactly what they do. Doing this in Japan [where Ronn was looking for new opportunities for P&G's dishwashing liquid], I could see for myself how cold the water was and exactly how [the target consumer] felt for greasy residue. Then when I asked to finish cleaning the dishes, she instructed me what to do. [Because he was] a foreigner and a man, she was certain I needed help and worked quite hard to improve my technique. None of the subtlety of this could ever be conveyed in a focus group.

Now every rule has an exception that proves it. If you want to find oversimplified consensus, a focus group's dynamics are perfect. This is why you see these groups all the time for political TV shows. Deep thinking is not what's being researched; rather, herd mentality is exactly what they are searching for. Out of context and forced to defend your point of view [when you are] unprepared in front of nine other people leads to shallow monologues about accepted beliefs. Sometimes that is what you are looking for.

I never got this banned at P&G. But it still should be. Whenever a focus group would do, there is a better technique that could be done instead and get you more for less.

You can find detailed tools to "do the job of discovering the job" in other books—notably *The Innovator's Guide to Growth*. That book has thousands of words on the topic. Or you could listen to five simple words from Steve Sharpe that echo Ronn's advice. I met Sharpe in 2006 during a project Innosight was doing with the American Press Institute to help newspaper organizations navigate through increasingly turbulent waters. At the time, Sharpe was the head of research for Media General, which owns a collective of media properties in the southeastern United States.[7] Sharpe led one of seven pilot projects we conducted with newspaper organizations to test some of the ideas we ended up recommending to the industry. We asked Sharpe—and the rest of the pilot participants—to describe the key lesson they learned from the project.

Sharpe's advice to the industry was succinct and useful: "Get out of the building." It's hard to discover new opportunities

---

7. I joined Media General's board of directors in April 2009.

when you are sitting at your desk; it's harder to understand what customers can't articulate if you don't spend time with them.

HOW-TO TIPS

- ✓ Spend an hour in a local coffee shop just watching how people go about their day. Write down three things you didn't expect.

- ✓ Ask your spouse or a friend to show you how they do an everyday task. Note two things that you see that you didn't expect.

Day 7
Don't Innovate Blind

Central Question	One-Sentence Answer
How can I confirm that the opportunity I have spotted is real?	Invest the time to understand the market you hope to target— always ask why smart people haven't seized an opportunity that looks obvious to you.

The goal of this first week's set of activities is to discover opportunities for innovation. The techniques described in the past six days should have helped you pinpoint a specific opportunity. But how can you be sure that you've actually identified something worth investigating further?

Sometimes it's useful to describe what *not* to do. And I'll use a Loony Tunes episode I remember from my childhood as a metaphor for the basic concept of avoiding *blind innovation*.

In said episode, Wile E. Coyote had a diabolical plan to get Bugs Bunny by inserting nitroglycerine into carrots. Bugs would take one bite of the carrot, and, boom, the end would be nigh.

Mr. Coyote was proud of his plan. "Wile E. Coyote, super genius," he intoned. "I like the way that rolls out." He cackled maniacally, unaware that Bugs had dragged the "laboratory" onto a train track. The train hits the shack, the nitroglycerine explodes, and the self-proclaimed super genius is left in his classic end-of-episode pose, holding on to a branch over an impossibly steep canyon.

Blind innovation occurs when innovators fall into the trap of believing that their sheer brilliance has allowed them to spot an opportunity that "lesser minds" have missed. This problem particularly afflicts managers in large, well-run companies. They look at other industries with a sneer of derision. "These guys are amateurs," they'll say. "We'll show them how it is really done."

For example, a couple of years ago, I was working with a project team that planned to create an infomercial to promote its product. The product was tailor-made for an infomercial, which is typically a thirty-minute interactive discussion led by an animated presenter like Ron Popeil or Anthony Sullivan on late-night television.[8] Because it took a bit of explanation to understand the product, it really helped to see the product in action to appreciate its potential benefits.

As the team members started exploring what the industry calls DRTV (for direct response television), they began to think about ways they could also pioneer a new-and-improved approach to infomercials.[9]

---

8. One of my favorite Malcolm Gladwell essays describes Ron Popeil. See Malcolm Gladwell, "The Pitchman," *New Yorker*, October 30, 2000, 64, www.gladwell.com/2000/2000_10_30_a_pitchman.htm.

9. *Direct response* refers to the infomercial's goal of getting people to call a phone number to order the product.

"These commercials are so amateurish," the team said. "We could produce something with much higher production values. Ours would be much more compelling than what is on the air now."

Fortunately, the team was working with a consultant who had significant experience in the DRTV industry. He scolded the team.

"You think these ads are low production quality because the people aren't smart?" he said. "It's the *exact opposite*. These people are brilliant at what they do. The commercials are the way they are because they've tested every approach known to man, and the seemingly amateurish approach generates the most sales. The apparent roughness makes the pitch feel more authentic, which helps to drive sales."

There's an important lesson in this example. The DRTV amateurs saw amateur commercials. The DRTV expert saw an optimized revenue-producing machine.

It is always good to start with a degree of humility. Instead of saying, "Why are the idiots doing it this way?" ask, "Why did smart people come up with this solution?" Or "What is it about this that I'm missing? It looks crazy to a non-expert!"

Innovators have to avoid the trap of getting stuck in endless analysis. But there are simple ways to determine if an apparent opportunity is a real opportunity.

One simple technique is to just pick up the phone and call someone who knows more about a particular problem than you do. The truth is, experts are almost always happy to talk about their area of expertise. And through university, professional, and personal networks, all of us are truly closer than ever before. There's simply no excuse for basing a business plan on an assumption that an expert could address in five minutes.

For example, we were helping a company develop a new business that involved selling to universities. The team assumed that it would take about three months for the company to close a deal with a university. That seemed kind of short to me. "Have any of you actually sold to a university before?" The answer was no. I suggested they might, you know, talk to someone who knew something about the industry. It took one phone call for the team to realize that the specific thing they hoped to sell would probably take three *years* to make it through the complicated purchasing process at universities. The telephone is a very much underrated research tool.

Another easy approach is to go on the Internet. This powerful democratizing force has reshaped a number of industries. It has given innovators an awesome wealth of tools and information. For example, when companies decide to issue stock to the public, the S-1 form they file with the Securities and Exchange Commission provides a wealth of data that can help anyone looking to innovate in similar industries. Reading through niche blog sites can provide tremendous information about the goings-on in an industry. Even company Web sites have lots of information about what companies will, and more importantly will not, do.

One final piece of advice. When conducting research, keep a running list of the things you don't know or aren't sure of. Those assumptions will come in handy in the third week of this book's training program.

Innovation is all about doing things differently, but that doesn't mean that innovators should be ignorant. Follow the advice of DNA pioneer James Watson and "never be the smartest person in the room"—humbly search out expertise to understand as much as possible about the areas you hope to explore, and most importantly, figure out the things you *don't* know.

Don't get me wrong; sometimes there is great value in bringing a new perspective to a problem. And we desperately need people who aren't satisfied by the status quo. But never, ever assume that the reason something hasn't happened is because of collective idiocy.

HOW-TO TIPS

✓ Look at the publicly available information about a large company you admire. Write down three things you didn't know.

✓ Call a friend, and have him or her spend fifteen minutes explaining how your friend's business really works.

Week 1 Wrap-Up

The focus of week 1 was discovering opportunities for innovation. Hopefully, the training helped you answer two critical questions:

1. What job is the target customer struggling to get done?
2. What evidence suggests that this is a real opportunity?

More broadly, remember three critical terms:

1. Job to be done: The problem facing a customer in a particular context
2. Nonconsumer: Someone who lacks the skills, wealth, or access to address a particular job to be done
3. Compensating behavior: A workaround that a customer follows to get a job done

BLUEPRINTING IDEAS

Coming up with ideas seems intimidating. Although Mike Tyson teaches us that our first idea is wrong in some meaningful way, it still helps to have as strong a starting point as possible. This week of innovation training draws on people such as Pablo Picasso and Dave Goulait to provide practical tips on how to develop a robust *blueprint*—or full schematic of what your idea will look like when you build it.

Make sure you start this week with a specific innovation opportunity. By the end of the week, you will have learned how to:

1. Draw on multiple sources of inspiration to develop an idea.

2. Determine where your idea can be "good enough."

3. Develop a comprehensive blueprint for your idea.

Day 8
Go to the Intersections

Central Question	One-Sentence Answer
How can I get inspiration for an idea?	Go to the intersections, and borrow liberally from other contexts.

Many people perceive that the hardest part of innovation is coming up with a new idea. After all, ideas are often represented by glowing light bulbs, representing a blinding, powerful, unforeseen insight.

But coming up with ideas is actually quite easy, if you remember Pablo Picasso's words of advice.

"Good artists copy," the Spanish painter noted. "Great artists steal."

In keeping with this theme, I liberally borrowed from David Kord Murray's helpful book *Borrowing Brilliance*. The book's basic theme is that the most reliable way to innovate is to borrow an idea from another field.

Murray suggests a simple, but useful process. You start by deeply understanding the problem you are trying to solve. Hopefully, you did this in week 1 of training! Then, determine who else has solved a similar problem—regardless of the field. Find ways to adapt the solution to the particulars of your problem. This technique dramatically simplifies one of the most daunting parts of the innovation process.

As an example, consider Rick Krieger. In the late 1990s, the Minneapolis-based entrepreneur and his partners saw an opportunity in the health-care industry. A bad emergency room visit led Krieger to observe that the health-care industry failed to deliver simple services in convenient, affordable ways. He thought about why that was the case. The problem was that the industry was designed to solve *any* problem. Skilled physicians were required to handle the complicated cases that *might* walk in the door.

Krieger asked himself which company had found ways to simplify a historically complicated delivery mechanism: bringing consistent quality, even with lesser-trained employees, lowering prices, improving convenience, and serving billions and billions of customers around the globe . . . Some of you probably have a crystal-clear image forming in your head: the international sign for fast food, McDonald's golden arches.

The next logical question, then, is, "What would a McDonald's of health care look like?"

McDonald's has simple, standardized menus; Krieger's solution would have to only offer a limited set of services. McDonald's has step-by-step instructions so that untrained teenagers can prepare food; Krieger would have to find a way to use lesser-skilled professionals.

In 2000, he and his partners introduced his business under the name QuickMedx. It was a seventy-five-square foot

A minuteClinic inside a CVS store in Massachusetts

kiosk staffed by a nurse practitioner. The practitioner could provide a range of straightforward services—think diagnosing strep throat or a flu shot—using simple, rules-based tests. QuickMedx promised that people would get in and out in fifteen minutes. The tagline? "You're sick. We're quick." In 2006, CVS Caremark bought the business—now branded MinuteClinic—for close to $200 million.

Here's a simple thought exercise to put this concept into action. Imagine you have identified a clear market need and have lined up a big meeting with an investor in a month. You have no money, but a shockingly high number of frequent flier miles. Assume black-out dates don't exist. Which company would you want to visit to get inspiration to build out your idea? Start researching that company immediately.

More generally, innovation scholars typically find that breakthrough innovation occurs at intersections when different fields, perspectives, or mind-sets collide. Jeffrey Dyer,

Hal Gregersen, and innovation master Clayton Christensen note in their 2011 book *The Innovator's DNA* how good innovators make these intersections happen by intentionally seeking out as many external stimuli as possible.

It sounds daunting, but it doesn't have to be. Four simple techniques can help you to find new perspectives:

1. Try to experience the new places you visit. If you happen to travel frequently for work, avoid the business traveler's rut of spending these trips in hotels and conference rooms. Seek out local dining establishments, or go eat in the company cafeteria. Local grocery stores can be a great window into how people really live their lives.

2. Learn about interesting individuals online. Maybe you've never been lucky enough to attend one of the famous gatherings sponsored by TED Conferences, so named for the nonprofit's focus on technology, entertainment, and design. (I've never been.) But you can "meet" a number of the TED attendees by watching the wide range of available videos. When you find someone who has an interesting perspective, try to learn as much as you can about the person. There is just an amazing amount of resources out on the Web.

3. Seek diversity in your reading. I rotate from business books to biographies to fiction to baseball books, sample from a pretty wide range of online and traditional publications, and even occasionally pick up some-

thing in a completely unrelated field. If your mind is programmed to think about innovation, you'll pick up surprising insights from material that seems to have nothing to do with your day job.

4. Always accept meetings with interesting people. Even if the meeting might seem like a distraction, take it. You are likely to get some nugget that pays dividends at some point.

These activities can seem disconnected from daily tasks, but they pay long-term dividends by programming the mind to make connections that it otherwise wouldn't make.

Innovation is a human-driven, social activity. Good innovators realize this and seek to make as many connections as they possibly can. If you are trying to think of your next great idea, remember Picasso and get yourself to the intersections.

HOW-TO TIPS

✓ Map out a three-day itinerary for places you could go to get nonobvious sources of inspiration.

✓ Watch an online video of one of the innovation masters in chapter 2. Write down one idea you take from the video.

✓ Send an e-mail to the most iconoclastic person you know, asking this person to introduce you to the most iconoclastic person *he or she* knows (unless that's you!).

Day 9
Seek Ideas from Everywhere

Central Question	One-Sentence Answer
Where should I look for inspiration?	Rapidly explore as many avenues as possible when searching for new ideas.

Despite time on my college newspaper and quite a few interviews with journalists, I don't consider myself particularly adept at the pithy sound bite. Every once in a while, however . . .

A couple of years ago, I was talking to a journalist about a contest Netflix was running. The company offered $1 million to any team that could help it offer significantly better DVD recommendations to its customers.[1]

The journalist asked me a question along the lines of "Do you think that it is better for companies to run these kinds of contests, or try to find ideas internally?"

My response? "I believe in monogamy in marriage and promiscuity in the search for new ideas."[2]

---

1. More than 250 teams entered the contest. Remarkably, the team that cracked the code was dispersed around the globe, and its members *had never met* until they received their check.

2. At least I think I said that. Google has no record of its ever being published. However, I did most definitely write about promiscuity in a 2009 blog and have used that line in speeches. See Scott D. Anthony, "My Best Innovation Advice? Be Promiscuous," hbr.org, September 23, 2009, http://blogs.hbr.org/anthony/2009/09/my_best_innovation_advice_be_p.html.

I went on to explain my belief that there is no one best source for new ideas. Instead, when you are trying to solve a tough problem, you should try to tackle the problem from as many perspectives as possible. Beyond the contest, I could see at least nine paths that Netflix could follow to come up with ideas to tackle the challenge of increasing the predictive nature of its algorithms by a certain percentage:

1. Form a small team (or several competing teams) of internal experts, and give them a defined period to come up with an idea.

2. Hire a specialist service provider, such as a company like ?Whatif! or Sagentia, to generate out-of-the-box ideas, or trawl through patent filings to get early reads on new technologies.

3. Challenge an intermediary like Innocentive, which attempts to match companies and individual problem solvers around the world.

4. Hold a half-day brainstorming session with a hand-picked group of outside experts.

5. Talk to a collection of venture capitalists who are investing in related start-ups.

6. Consider a strategic partnership with an early-stage company in the space.

7. Have a team do day 8's training, and look for relevant analogies from different industries.

8. Solicit suggestions from loyal Netflix customers (preferably using the excellent research and writing from members of the open-innovation community).

9. Conduct an ethnographic study to identify nonobvious ways that customers today solve the content-discovery process.

Some of these clearly would be harder to pull off. For example, loyal customers (number eight on the list above) probably lack the technological sophistication to offer particularly useful solutions. But you never know unless you try. And there are a raft of excellent resources for people who want to explore these different approaches (e.g., check out Stefan Lindegaard's excellent 15inno network, at www.15inno.com).

At first glance, the list above might seem a bit overwhelming, but the search for inspiration doesn't have to be overly complicated. Start by researching how other people have solved similar problems. Thankfully, Google has made this process blissfully easy! Find ways to talk to people who might offer inspiration. Friends, family, and colleagues always serve as good starting points. Don't be afraid to contact people whom you don't know but whom you come across while doing research. People generally love to talk about the things they have accomplished.

If you find yourself stuck staring at a blank piece of paper, ask simple what-if questions, such as these:

- What if I did the same thing this other smart person did? Remember yesterday's lesson: there is no shame in borrowing someone else's brilliant idea.

- What if I were the CEO of a company I admire? How would he or she solve this problem?

- What if I combined two seemingly unconnected ideas?

The goal is to develop a list of the different ideas that begin to pop into your mind. Initial ideas don't have to be overly polished; a single sentence description or a rough sketch can be sufficient. Ideally, each idea represents what strategists call *pure tones*. That is, the ideas have a meaningful and noticeable difference from other ideas on your list.

One other tip: carry around something that allows you to capture inspiration when it strikes. This used to require something burdensome like a small notebook, but of course, today you can use your smartphone to jot short notes to yourself, take snapshots, or record movies.

It is important to remember that in this part of the process the goal isn't to come up with a single idea; it is to come up with lots of ideas. Why is that? Look up to Mike Tyson on the Mount Rushmore of Innovation, and remember that your first idea is going to be wrong in some meaningful way. If you generate a lot of ideas, you might find ways to combine ideas to come up with something you hadn't thought of before.

Many view innovation as a solitary pursuit, but it shouldn't be. Cast as wide a net as possible to get inspiration that translates into tangible innovation ideas. As my wife says, "This is one time when I approve of promiscuity!"

HOW-TO TIPS

✓ Create a list of ways you could approach a problem that has been nagging you for weeks; make the list as long as possible.

✓ Call up an entrepreneur or an artist and ask how he or she comes up with ideas. Try this person's techniques.

Day 10
Remember: Quality Is Relative

Central Question	One-Sentence Answer
Is my idea high quality?	Quality is a relative term that can only be determined by understanding what matters to the target customer.

The previous two days of training suggested sources of inspiration for innovative ideas. Hopefully, the techniques allowed you to develop the beginning of an idea to do something different that will have impact. The next few days will help you transform an emerging idea into a more detailed blueprint. Today's training helps you think about what makes your idea special.

Would-be innovators often trip over the word *quality*. The basic problem? People often think their definition of quality is the same as their customer's definition of quality. That is rarely the case. If you want to develop a compelling idea, look again at A. G. Lafley's face on our Mount Rushmore of innovation, and remember to look at the world through your customer's eyes.

This notion hit home to me right after my family and I moved to Singapore. For those of you who haven't spent time in Singapore, the country is just food mad. You can find every kind of food imaginable. Locals will tell you that the best food comes from stalls at so-called hawker centers. The stalls are basically small kiosks manned by one or two people who churn out fresh, affordable food.

These aren't the "roach coaches" that populate the streets of New York City. In true Singaporean fashion, the food stalls are regulated. Each stall has a highly visible laminated card showing how well it adheres to published cleanliness standards.

I had visited tons of stalls on my trips to Singapore and was a big fan of the food. So, after we touched down, I was excited to bring this innovative offering to my wife.[3] Great, affordable food from a stall! What's not to love?

Now, my wife loves good food as much as the next person. One of our favorite things to do is to explore new restaurants. She's willing to try just about anything.

But I knew something wasn't right when we went to a well-known outdoor hawker center. Joanne picked at her food and made obligatory comments about how it was great; she just wasn't hungry because of the jet lag.

Later, it hit me. While I would very happily trade off a bit of ambience for freshness and food quality, my wife's preferences were completely reversed. A restaurant needed to cross a certain ambiance threshold to be of interest to her. If it fell below that threshold, three Michelin stars wouldn't tempt her palate.

---

3. My wife had never visited Singapore before we moved out in 2010. She is brave, mostly for trusting me to find a place to live.

When I asked her about it afterward, she said, "You know, I was worried I wasn't going to eat for the next few years. The food was good, but I just couldn't get over seeing all the cooked chickens and ducks that are on display."

The problem again was I had assumed she would rate quality the same way I would. But she didn't.

Here's another example from Singapore. Look at my picture on the jacket flap. Check out my hairstyle. Ask yourself, "What does Scott look for in a haircut?"

The only haircut that would be simpler than mine would be a military-grade buzz cut. Typically, I tell the barber, "Two, three, four," describing the length of blade I use in the back, middle, and top of my head.

Yet, somehow in America, I couldn't find a good, reliable place to get my hair cut. The local Supercuts had shockingly variable quality. The nearest salon would be more reliable, but really, paying $50 for *this* haircut just seemed . . . wrong. In the end, we worked out a system where I would go to Supercuts and get a fairly mediocre haircut, and then Joanne would do a bit of a touch-up at home. Seems a bit much for *this*.

Then, when we arrived in Singapore, my colleague told me about QB House. The company's slogan is "10 Minutes, Just Cut." Each location has about four barber chairs. A light outside the location and connected to sensors to chairs for waiting customers tells you the length of the queue. You put a $10 note into a vending machine and get a card. You hand that card to a barber, and he or she gets to work. The place only does haircuts—no shampoos, no eyebrow shaping, and no coloring. Just cuts. Each chair has in front of it a television monitor that plays television commercials so you don't have to pretend to make small talk with the barber. Hygiene is clearly important, as you can visibly see the alcohol in which the scissors are sanitized. After you are done, an integrated vacuum machine sucks up the clippings.

Now, if my hair looked like the mane on Russell Brand, I would view QB House as a not very good solution. But for me, QB House is pretty close to heaven. It is predictable, it is clean, it is affordable, and it is simple.

Both of these examples highlight how quality is a relative term. You have to understand individuals and what matters to them before you determine whether something is a high- or low-quality idea. Of course, you have to be better than what the customer could historically access or afford along *some* dimensions. But being good enough on other dimensions often opens up new innovation opportunities.

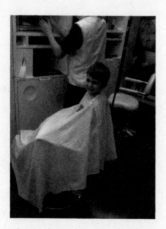

Charlie Anthony, enjoying a QB House haircut.

There are a number of useful tools to help visualize the performance customers are seeking on a range of dimensions. One of the most helpful ones I've found is the *strategy canvas* from W. Chan Kim and Renée Mauborgne's *Blue Ocean Strategy*. In essence the canvas lists the performance dimensions on one axis and shows how different solutions measure up against each dimension.

We use a variant of this canvas in our consulting work quite frequently, because it addresses two key innovation issues. First, it can help you understand where there is opportunity to do something different when the existing solutions aren't providing something that a population is looking for. Second, a strategy canvas can help you understand whether your idea will have an impact on the target audience. If you are providing bells and whistles that don't matter and that are falling short of key thresholds, you are likely to disappoint.

Joanne is getting more used to the food stalls, by the way.

HOW-TO TIPS

- ✓ Ask failed sales prospects or lapsed customers to detail criteria they used to make a decision.

- ✓ Ask a dining companion how food quality, ambience, and service affect his or her view of a restaurant.

- ✓ Google "strategy canvas"—create one for an innovative idea on which you are working.

Day 11
Avoid Overshooting

Central Question	One-Sentence Answer
Is there such a thing as too good?	It is possible to overshoot your target market by introducing features that the customer will take, but not value enough to pay for.

There are a few popular catchphrases within the Anthony family. My grandfather used to say, "You make a better door than a window" to a person standing between him and the television. When asked whether he liked a meal, my dad has been known to declare, "It sung with the goodness of the sun-drenched earth."[4] When asked about how an event went, the expected answer is, "A good time was had by all!" My mother's contribution? "You can never be too rich or too thin."

That last one may be true, but when it comes to innovation, you can in fact be too good.

---

4. My father was also the creator of the ill-fated Darwin's Drill. He would go to the back porch with a plate of leftovers, yell "Darwin's Drill!," and throw the food into the backyard. The strongest got the food. The weakest went hungry. My mother didn't let this one last.

The innovation literature suggests that surprisingly, at some time in the life cycle of any product or service, customers no longer value incremental improvements. Existing customers will almost always *take* something better (unless it gets too complex), but at some point, they become disinterested in paying for it. Innovation master Christensen termed this *overshooting*.

When I am working with a group, I will introduce the concept of overshooting by going through something like the following: "The telephone service in your house is a technological marvel. The quality is so clear, that companies tell you that you can hear a pin drop. You have 'five nines' reliability, meaning your phone works 99.999 percent of the time, or all but five minutes a year. There's even an electrical current running over your wire, which means even if the power is out in your neighborhood, your phone still works."

I then go on to pitch a new service offering from the local phone company to the group: "Have we got a deal for you! Our engineers have introduced next-generation sound quality. It's so clear that you can hear a pin whooshing through the air. We will give you that elusive *sixth* nine. That's right, that's a downtime of only thirty-one seconds a year. Electrical currents are passé. We'll throw in a *personal generator* to make sure your phone is always powered."

If I'm on my game, I've got the audience at this point. Then, it's time for the kicker: "So my question for you is this: How many of you would pay a price premium for this service?"

I've never had someone seriously say yes to this question. You would *take* that new-and-improved service, of course.

But you wouldn't pay price premiums for it—certainly not with affordable, convenient options like mobile phones, Skype, and so on.

Now this is obviously an edge condition. But the general phenomenon is real. There is such a thing as too good. At some point, the cost required to deliver incremental improvements doesn't match the benefit that customers would derive from the improvement.

The discussion of the innovation sin of pride in chapter 4 noted how razor leader Gillette seemed to be on the brink of overshooting. A 2008 *Wall Street Journal* article, "Gillette Sharpens Its Pitch for Expensive Razor," by Ellen Byron in fact showed early warning signs of this occurring, despite the successful launch of Gillette's five-blade Fusion razor.

Most notably, people were hesitating to upgrade to new products. One analyst told the *Journal*, "When you went from [Gillette's] Atra to Sensor, or Sensor to Mach3, practically everyone changed their razor. But with Fusion, you're getting to such high price points that it actually makes a difference in their shopping basket—how much closer can your shave really get and how much closer does it need to be?"

Further, unit sales of low-cost, no-brand products were taking off. The *Journal* article described how Information Resources, Inc. (IRI), data (which does not include Walmart) showed that Gillette's unit sales had sagged between 2007 and 2008, whereas private label units had increased 11 percent.

Those are the kinds of developments that signal overshooting. The historical pattern would lead to Gillette's suffering from declining growth and the emergence of game-changing solutions that play the shaving game differently.

The folks at Gillette (and its corporate parent, Procter & Gamble) are pretty bright. In 2010, Gillette introduced the Fusion ProGlide system. Instead of simply adding another blade, the company sought to make the product much easier to use. It was a smart move, given industry trends. Also in 2010, Gillette went in the complete opposite direction by introducing the Gillette Guard—a 15-rupee razor—in India (that's about 33 cents). The company also sought to bring its brand to personal care products like shampoos and body washes.

Gillette seems to be following Intel's playbook. During the 1990s, the chip manufacturer competed almost entirely on the basis of the speed of its processors. Over the past decade, it shifted to focus on dimensions such as battery life and wireless performance and to move into new categories like education, health care, and television.

These examples show that, as is the case for many innovation concepts, overshooting is both a threat and an opportunity. A company that overshoots a market can see its core business crumble pretty quickly. For example, in 1996, Kodak rolled out its Advanced Picture System (APS) film, which promised the ability to take pictures of various sizes and to produce even higher-quality prints. However, it turned out that people were perfectly satisfied with lower-quality but easier-to-share digital images. Kodak shut down APS in 2004.

Overshooting is an opportunity because it creates conditions favoring innovative approaches to compete in a marketplace. Instead of seeking to leapfrog existing solutions, innovators can be on the lookout for ways to make things simpler or easier to use. They should ask provocative questions such as "What would happen if we removed 90 percent of the features and functions in our existing offerings? Would it allow price points to get to the level where an unserved market would be reachable? Could the offering be simplified to the point where non-experts could do it themselves?"

For the curious, I actually have no idea whether any phone company is working on that sixth nine. My market research suggests that the number of people who will pay for that feature is precisely zero.

HOW-TO TIPS

✓ Run a thought experiment to see what would happen if you or the market leader cut features by 20 percent and prices by 80 percent.

✓ Pick a product from your kitchen cabinet. Identify three improvements that would be exciting to designers or engineers, but useless to you.

Day 12
Do It Differently

Central Question	One-Sentence Answer
What is a disruptive innovation?	Disruptive innovations create new markets and transform existing ones through simplicity, convenience, affordability, or accessibility.

Almost every organization that has changed in a meaningful way has a Dave Goulait. I first met Goulait in 2004, when he was the point person for our work with Procter & Gamble. His job was to help P&G improve its innovation productivity. Over the next few years, we worked closely with Goulait to help P&G build a corporate capability to create new-growth businesses. Goulait retired in 2007, seamlessly passing the baton to a hand-chosen successor. Goulait is self-admittedly not very good at retirement, so after formally retiring, he did part-time contracting work for P&G and Innosight.

Why was Goulait such a powerful corporate change agent? He focused 100 percent of his energy on getting P&G to change and zero percent of his energy on building the "Goulait brand." So, it seems appropriate to recognize Goulait in today's training, as one of his favorite principles provides a good way to make several key points about *disruptive innovation*, a powerful weapon that would-be innovators can use to develop high-potential opportunities.

Goulait's principle? "To do something different, you have to do something different."

It's almost Einsteinian in its simplicity (and, perhaps unintentionally, it channeled Einstein's definition of insanity—following the same behavior and expecting different results).

The Dave Goulait innovation principle points inexorably to disruptive innovation. If your mission is to shake up the establishment or to create what doesn't exist, then you simply can't do the same thing that everyone else is doing. You have to find a way to do what people *aren't* doing, or to take a radically different approach to the status quo.

Christensen popularized the term *disruptive innovation* in his 1997 bestseller *The Innovator's Dilemma*.[5] At its core, a disruptive innovation is something that creates a new market or transforms an existing one through simplicity, convenience, accessibility, or affordability.

Two classic examples of disruptive innovation are the personal computer and discount retailers. Personal computers democratized their market. Back in the 1970s, only trained experts could use computers. Existing technology (minicomputers and mainframes) were only affordable to large

---

5. *The Innovator's Dilemma* actually used the term *disruptive technology*, but Christensen defined technology in such an expansive way that he appropriately rebranded the concept *disruptive innovation* in later writing. Christensen will now privately admit regret for using the word *disruptive*, as people often confuse what he intended by this term with common dictionary definitions.

corporations. The net result was that most people didn't consume much computing technology. As Apple and other innovators made things simpler and more affordable, they created an entirely new industry. Ultimately, that industry grew big enough to marginalize many of the computing titans of the 1970s and 1980s.

Discount retailers emerged in the United States after World War II. Historically, leading department store retailers featured a range of high-quality goods and well-trained salespeople who guided purchase decisions. Discount retailers offered simpler products that sold themselves. By reducing overhead, Walmart and other discounters could offer much lower price points.

Disruption has affected dozens of industries—high tech, low tech, business to business, business to consumer, service based, and product based.[6] There are always nuances, but the basic story is eerily similar.

It starts with an innovator developing something with good-enough raw performance and improved simplicity or accessibility or lower prices. The innovator introduces the product or service outside the mainstream market. Perhaps

---

6. One thing we should create but haven't is the gold standard "disruptive database" that lists every certified disruptive development we can find. *The Innovator's Solution* had a pretty comprehensive list of developments up until about 2000. We produced a special issue of our newsletter in 2007 to celebrate the tenth anniversary of the publication of *The Innovator's Dilemma* highlighting more recent developments. Highlights from that special issue can be found in Clayton Christensen and Innosight, "Decade of Disruption," *Forbes.com*, October 26, 2007, www.forbes.com/2007/08/31/christensen-disruption-kodak-pf-guru_in_cc_0904christensen_inl.html.

it is to an undemanding customer who is happy to trade performance for price. Perhaps it is to a customer who historically lacked the skills or wealth to use existing solutions. The innovator uses this foothold to improve the product and service so that it meets the needs of broader customer groups. An innovation that was once dismissed as inferior becomes perfectly adequate for wider use.

Historically, the innovators who mastered disruptive innovation would come from outside an industry's mainstream. That's why Christensen called his first book *The Innovator's Dilemma*. He observed how many historically great companies—such as Kodak, Digital Equipment Corporation, Sears, and General Motors—stumbled by doing precisely what they were supposed to do. That is, they listened to their most important customers, innovated to meet those customers' needs, pushed prices and margins up—and suffered a stunning defeat at the hand of a seemingly innocent attacker armed with a disruptive innovation. As Christensen and colleagues have further decoded disruption, an increasing number of market leaders, like Cisco Systems, Procter & Gamble, and the Tata Group, are using disruptive innovation to their advantage.

You can use disruptive innovation to further develop your idea. What would it look like if you dramatically *lowered* performance on what people considered to be the *most* important dimension of performance? Don't think this means introducing something crummy. Rather, think about how this approach could allow you to make something simpler or more affordable.

Remember, disruptive innovation is a tool. I have seen some people get so obsessed with fitting Christensen's definition of disruption that they forget to ask basic questions, like "Does anyone want this?" or "Will we be able to charge high enough prices to cover our costs?" Always remember that the business of business is business. Thinking disruptively can point you in new directions, but never forget that the ultimate destination is impact.

Nonetheless, when developing an innovative idea remember the Dave Goulait innovation principle—to do something different, you have to do something different.

HOW-TO TIPS

- ✓ Identify an item that you use every day and that followed the pattern of disruptive innovation.

- ✓ If you are working on an innovative idea, write down three changes you could make to it to make it more closely fit the disruptive pattern.

- ✓ Identify three startups that could have disruptive impact on your industry.

Day 13
Embrace Business Model Innovation

Central Question	One-Sentence Answer
What is a business model, and how do I innovate it?	A business model describes how a company creates, captures, and delivers value; systematically considering a wide range of business model options can help enable business model innovation.

Quick—name the most successful technology companies from the first decade of the twenty-first century. If you are like a lot of people, the names that typically come to mind are Google, Amazon, Netflix, and Apple.[7] It's a pretty good collection. If you had invested $10,000 in Apple and Amazon on December 31, 1999, and $10,000 more in Netflix and Google when they went public in 2002 and 2004, respectively, by the end of 2009, you would have had a tidy $230,000,

---

7. Unless you live in Asia, in which case you would probably have noted Tencent or Baidu, both of which also fit this pattern.

compared with $37,500 if you had invested the same amount in the NASDAQ index on the same dates.

What do these companies have in common? You might at first think, "They invest a lot of money in technology," but one nonobvious connection is that the key to each of their successes is their *business model.*

Look at Apple and Amazon in particular. Apple introduced a series of legitimately game-changing technologies during the 2000s, most notably its portable music player and its smartphone. Clever, powerful operating systems powered both of those platforms. However, in both cases, the true driver of success was unique business models. Think of what would have happened if Apple had not coupled the iPod with easy-to-use software and a music store that offered songs at the unheard-of price of $0.99. Or if Apple had never created the App Store, which as of this book's writing had more than 300,000 applications people could run on their iPhone.[8] Or if Apple hadn't created its own retail stores, which by 2011 sold more than $1 billion worth of products . . . a month.

Amazon is a *serial* business model innovator. Its core model is very innovative. If you tear apart its financial statements, the company doesn't look like a retailer. Instead, it looks like a company that sells magazine subscriptions. How is that? Amazon has organized its business so that it initiates a purchase order with its supplier *after* you place your order.

---

8. My five-year-old son is partial to *Angry Birds* and *Cut the Rope*. My three-year-old daughter likes *Sundae Maker*.

It pays the supplier fifteen to thirty days in the future. So it gets your money before it pays the supplier. It's like you purchased a subscription that Amazon fulfills over time. This allows Amazon to have negative days working capital, which is quite rare for a retailer! When Amazon expanded from its original core of book retailing into other product categories, it became a general-purpose retailer. It then went into subscription services with its Amazon Prime offering, where the company offers customers the ability to avoid shipping charges by paying an annual fee. It rightly bet that the increase in purchase volume would offset any loss resulting from free shipping. Amazon is also a leading provider of *cloud computing services*, whereby small businesses essentially rent capabilities from Amazon instead of buying proprietary hardware. In 2008, it introduced the first version of its Kindle e-reader. As other companies—most notably Apple—introduced competing devices, Amazon created software offerings that allowed consumers to continue to get Kindle-based books on any platform. Not everything has succeeded (auctions, for example, were a bit of a dud), but it's an impressive ten-year oeuvre.

Of course, without whiz-bang technologies, any of these companies would fizzle. But the best innovators go well beyond thinking about the features or functions of their product or service. They think about innovative ways to develop an end-to-end business model.

Now, a business model is a term that gets thrown around a lot without a clear definition. Innosight's definition of a business model—spelled out in Mark Johnson's *Seizing the White*

Space—is "the blueprint that defines the way a company delivers value to a set of customers at a profit." Johnson's framework suggests looking at three things:

1. How you create value. Think beyond the solution itself to where the customers find the solution, how they obtain it, and so on.

2. How you capture value. Are there different ways to make money?

3. How you deliver value. What are you doing yourself, and what are partners doing? How are you doing the work? What could you do differently?

A good idea blueprint results from thinking carefully through each of these areas. I'll use a family story to illustrate the array of choices innovators should consider.

In 2000, my sister Michelle was pursuing a PhD in developmental psychology from the University of California–Berkeley. Her particular focus was the role of American Sign Language in language acquisition, cognition, and literacy. One interesting thing she had discovered was that the desire to communicate occurred before throat muscles matured enough to support speech. When she had her first daughter that year, she wondered about teaching her to communicate using American Sign Language.

As my sister delved deeper into the subject, she learned that research suggested that children who learned to sign enjoyed a statistically significant and lasting IQ boost. The theory held that once kids learned that communication led to desirable results, they were hungry for more. Of course, once the throat muscles developed, hearing children learned that speech is more efficient than sign to communicate with hearing parents and siblings, so the use of sign language gradually decreases.

My sister also learned that the books on the subject were either academic but inaccessible, or were accessible but lacked rigor. She saw an opportunity for a structured approach that also was parent friendly. So she worked with a friend to create a business capitalizing on her insight.

Think about the choices facing my sister.

How could she create value? At the core of her idea was a simple methodology. She could spread that methodology through tools like flashcards, videos, in-person courses, or online videos. She could distribute products herself, through third-party retailers like Amazon, or through partners like Gymboree or Kindermusik.

How could she capture value? She could obviously capitalize on direct sales to consumers. She could also license her products and services to other resellers or charge franchise fees to local entrepreneurs who wanted to run their own play classes.

How could she deliver value? She could build up a team of salespeople and product designers or look for partners to help scale the business. She could try to build her own brand or try to partner with other popular brands. She could market by building a Web site, use more grassroots outreach on blogs and other forms of social media, or advertise in traditional media channels.

Whew!

My sister chose to brand the offering Signing Smart. She focused on selling videos and training tools through Web-based and direct channels and offered training courses through a partnership with Kindermusik, which has a network of more than five thousand educators providing early learning through music and movement (her program—Sign and Sing, developed by Signing Smart—is still offered by Kindermusik). While commercial results to date have been relatively modest, her thoughtful approach gave her a platform, learning, and a following. In 2010, she leveraged this when she wrote *Little Girls Can Be Mean*, the first book to provide practical guidance about how to bully-proof elementary-aged girls.[9] As I'll explain in week 3, every innovation success story has some twists and turns along the way!

My sister may never reach the levels of Apple, Amazon, or Google. But thinking comprehensively through her business model choices increased the chance that she'll end up successfully creating, capturing, and delivering value.

HOW-TO TIPS

✓ Document the business model of your company or idea (there are useful tools available at www.seizingthewhitespace.com or at Alexander Oster-walder's businessmodelgeneration.com).

---

9. Michelle Anthony and Reyna Lindert, *Little Girls Can Be Mean: Four Steps to Bully-Proof Girls in the Early Grades* (New York: St. Martin's Griffin, 2010).

✓ Map out your personal business model—how do you create, capture, and deliver value in your life?

✓ Identify a business model you admire. What would it look like if you merged that business model with the idea you have been working on?

Day 14
Bring It Together

Central Question	One-Sentence Answer
How can I translate my work into a concrete blueprint?	"Don't just do something—stand there"; step back and summarize your work in a comprehensive plan.

In 2009, we had a small gathering in which we brought together senior leaders from a range of companies to talk privately about their issues with growth and innovation. During that meeting, innovation master Richard Foster presented his latest thinking on the topic. It was a tour de force—one hundred PowerPoint slides in an hour, with rich historical examples, funny stories, and quirky case studies. The part I remember most clearly—and the final component of week 2's training—was Foster's guidance about how to be a better innovative thinker: "Don't just do something. Stand there."

Read that again. Foster explained that it was important to not just get caught up in the daily grind of activities. Rather, innovators need to be able to piece together their work into a comprehensive plan. Generally, there are four levels at which you can synthesize the work that has preceded this activity:

1. The elevator pitch: How would you describe your idea in sixty seconds or less?

2. The idea résumé: How can you describe your idea on a single piece of paper?[10]

3. The executive summary: What are five to ten Power-Point slides (or equivalent) that describe the essence of your idea?

4. The detailed blueprint: What precisely do you plan to do, why will it work, and why does it matter?

While the pithier summaries contained in levels 1 through 3 are important tools to help summarize and sell ideas (more on the importance of that sales process next week), this day's training will focus on the more comprehensive level 4 blueprint.

There is no one-size-fits-all approach to this blueprint. A new-growth business blueprint, for example, will look very different from a process improvement blueprint. I usually advise corporate clients and entrepreneurs to cover at least the following elements of the blueprint:[11]

---

10. *The Innovator's Guide to Growth*, chapter 5, has an example of an idea résumé.

11. If any of the terms in the list are unfamiliar, check out Howard Stevenson et al., *The Entrepreneurial Venture*, 2nd ed., Practice of Management Series (Boston: Harvard Business School Press, 1999); or Robert Higgins, *Analysis for Financial Management*, 9th ed. (New York: McGraw-Hill, 2008). You can also get some general definitions from Wikipedia.

- The target customer: What job is the customer struggling to get done? What suggests that the job is important and unsatisfied?

- Key stakeholders: Who else is involved in the decision to purchase and use an offering? What are their jobs to be done? Why will they support the idea?

- The idea: How will the idea ease the customer's pain? How does it compare to other ways the customer could get the job done? What makes it different and better? What will it look and feel like?

- The economics: What revenues will be earned? What is the cost of earning those revenues? What infrastructure will be required? What capital expenditures are required?

- The commercialization path: What is the foothold market where you will start? What is the plan to expand from the foothold?

- Operations: What are the key activities involved in the opportunity? Who is doing what? What will you do? What partnerships will you need to form? What will you need to acquire?

- The team: Who is on the team? Why do you believe that this team has any chance of succeeding?

- The financing: How much money is required to execute the plan? How long will it take to earn a return on that money? Who has funded the business to date? What have they provided?

- The action plan: What are the most critical assumptions? What are the near-term activities to learn more about those assumptions?

In week 3, you will get further detail on how to think about some of the elements above, notably the economics and the action plan. But for now, this list helps you to consider your idea from multiple perspectives. Run through what-if questions, like "What if we targeted this customer?" or "What if we doubled our price?" or "What if our rival bought this hot start-up that we are eyeing?" Look at your idea through the eyes of partners, suppliers, distribution channels, and so on. One good way to fail is to violate a simple but important rule: people don't do what doesn't make sense to them. A surprising number of companies rest success on asking a sales channel to change its model, or a supplier to lose money, or a partner to sign an obviously one-sided deal. These thought exercises should help you develop a more robust idea and flag key assumptions that you need to address in next week's exercises.

Innovation is an iterative process. An innovator should always be researching *and* developing an idea *and* testing. Good innovators have to step back and integrate what they are learning from their research, experiments, and connections. They should be able to understand what that learning means and incorporate it into their idea. So this day's lesson—bring it all together—is one that could have appeared in any of the first three weeks and is one that you can and should return to frequently.

HOW-TO TIPS

✓ Develop a sixty-second elevator pitch for an idea that you've been working on. Present that pitch to a friend.

✓ Ask an entrepreneur or a small-business owner you know for a copy of their business plan.

✓ Visit slideshare.com and look for good examples of business plans.

Week 2 Wrap-Up

The focus of week 2 was blueprinting an innovative idea. You hopefully answered three critical questions:

1. What is the essence of my innovative idea? What is different? Why will it have impact?

2. Where will it be better than what the customer can access or afford today? Where will it be good enough?

3. What is my comprehensive plan?

More broadly, remember four critical phrases:

1. Brilliant borrowing: identifying which people or other groups have already solved your problem, wherever in the world they might be

2. Disruptive innovation: something that creates a new market or transforms an existing one through simplicity, convenience, accessibility, or affordability

3. Good enough: a simple way to capture the notion that sacrificing raw performance can open up new innovation options

4. Business model: how you create, capture, and deliver value

WEEK 3

ASSESSING AND
TESTING IDEAS

There's a misbegotten sense that the biggest hurdle facing the would-be innovator is developing a winning idea. Ideas are actually the relatively easy part. The hard part is actually doing something with the idea. This week of innovation training draws on Indian barbers, a software titan, and Thomas Edison to help you identify whether your idea does in fact have potential and to help you run experiments to address critical unknowns.

This week will help you to accomplish the following tasks:

1. Assess the potential of your idea.

2. Identify the biggest assumptions behind realizing that potential.

3. Design experiments to address those assumptions.

4. Draw the right implications from those experiments.

Day 15
Let Patterns Guide
and Actions Decide

Central Question	One-Sentence Answer
How can I separate good ideas from bad ideas?	Use patterns to get a directional sense as to whether an idea is any good, and then run experiments to confirm that directional sense.

If you accept the teachings from Mike Tyson, Helmut von Moltke, and Rita McGrath in chapter 3, you accept that the idea that you worked on diligently in week 2 is wrong in some meaningful way. The critical issue, then, is identifying whether there's at least hope that you could be moving in a productive direction.

So how can you tell whether an idea does in fact have potential? I know how most large companies approach this problem. They break out the spreadsheets. They ask innovators to create models projecting the potential of their idea. The model spits out a number—perhaps a net present value or a return on investment. The higher the number, the greater the chance that management will take the idea forward.

Courtesy of Intuit

Scott Cook

The approach is a reasonable enough way to compare projects with a high degree of certainty. After all, you can believe the assumptions in the analysis on the spreadsheet. But when you are innovating—particularly if you are doing something that hasn't been done before—the numbers can be deceiving.

Scott Cook is the founder and chairman of Intuit, whose claim to fame is TurboTax, Quicken, and QuickBooks. These programs all bring financial discipline to users. Cook is also the source of perhaps my favorite quote about innovation: "For every one of our failures, we had spreadsheets that looked awesome."

Don't ever confuse an awesome spreadsheet with an awesome business. They are two different things.

On the flip side, sometimes a terrible spreadsheet can obscure a good business. Consider the case example of Align.[1] I first met this team in 2004 during a workshop we were doing for Procter & Gamble. The team was developing

---

1. To those few souls who are regular readers, I do apologize for using this story so frequently. It has the double advantage of being a legitimately good story and one for which I actually have approval to go into the nitty-gritty details.

a probiotic supplement whose daily use could alleviate the symptoms of irritable bowel syndrome. More than 30 million people in the United States alone suffer from this condition. The best that most of the afflicted can do is to modify their lives to account for their condition.

The idea was brimming with disruptive potential. It addressed a pressing problem with no adequate solutions. And it proposed a potentially category-creating way to get the job done. The product had unique intellectual property, and consumers who tried it literally reported that their lives changed.

And, of course, it was about to get shut down.

Why the disconnect? The original market forecast said that the opportunity would be relatively small. Launching a new brand is expensive, and the team hadn't yet worked out all the technological kinks. Big investment, high risk, small return, is not a recipe for corporate approval.

Yet, the Align team persevered. It turned out the critical factor in the market research was the degree to which customers would take the pill every day (in industry language, *compliance*). Consumers told researchers that they would probably take the pill occasionally. Of course, since consumers had never experienced the benefit, there was a reasonable chance that their self-reported figure didn't reflect reality. The team conducted scenario analysis to identify what compliance would have to look like to justify a full-scale launch. Management agreed to follow more of a venture-capital approach, where the company would provide a small amount of seed capital to learn more about these assumptions. The team quietly launched the product over the Internet. It didn't spend tens of millions in national advertising; rather it conducted targeted activities in a handful of cities. It turned out compliance in the controlled pilot was high enough to warrant expanding distribution to include Web sites like Walgreens.com. Further progress led to a national launch in 2009. The product won a coveted industry award as the most innovative launch in its category.

So, if good spreadsheets can obscure a crummy business, and crummy spreadsheets can obscure a good business, what do you do?

On the basis of his experience, Cook has developed a simple rule of thumb: he guides teams to assess the depth of the customer need and the novelty of their solution. His experience teaches him that getting those two things right typically lays the foundation of successful new businesses. Align certainly passed those two tests! I generally ask five questions of any entrepreneur with an idea:

1. Is there an *important problem* that customers can't address because existing solutions are expensive or inconvenient? In the language of this book, is there a high-potential job to be done?

2. Is there a *disruptive* way to solve the problem in a simpler, more convenient, or more affordable way?

3. Is there a *plausible hypothesis* about an economically attractive, scalable business model? Answering this question doesn't require a detailed financial model (which is wrong, anyway), but it does require a sensible story that's at least conceivable—and a plan to turn that hypothesis into reality. (Day 16's training

describes how to come up with a quick view of an idea's financial potential.)

4. Does the team have the *right stuff* to course-correct according to in-market learning? Remember, the odds are high that the first idea isn't quite right. A team that is dogmatic and keeps trying to prove it is right is the wrong team for many innovation efforts.

5. Can *early profitability* be a choice? Ultimate success requires a profitable model. The sooner there is a line of sight to profits, the better. You might make a strategic decision to be unprofitable by investing in marketing, sales capability, and so on, but at least you know that the core part of the model works.

In both cases, Cook and I are relying on patterns. That's not to say these are the only patterns or the best ones for different contexts. But the general guidance holds—if you are trying to figure out if your idea, approach, or plan has merit, go back and look at history. Look at what you or other people tried. What worked or what didn't? For example, if you are trying to determine if you have enough savings to go back and get a doctoral degree, and your projections say you are going to write your thesis 50 percent faster than anyone in history, at least ask the question, "What does history teach us?"[2]

---

2. It turns out, sadly, that human beings are pretty bad at doing this. The literature calls it *planning fallacy*. We always think things will be quicker and cheaper than they are. We do indeed live in Lake Wobegon, where all the people think they are above average.

Let patterns guide . . . but let actions decide. The truth is that even something that fits a pattern perfectly can fail. Look up to Mike Tyson's face on the Mouth Rushmore of Innovation to remember that you *are* going to be punched in the face. Something is undoubtedly wrong about your idea. And you have to figure out what is wrong. The only way you know whether you have a good idea is when someone pays money for your product or service, when the amount that someone pays supports a profitable business model, when you actually start to achieve the results you had hoped for, and so on.

That doesn't mean you have to place a big bet or wait a long time to qualify an idea. Your goal is to learn as much as you can as quickly as you can by running focused experiments. Hungry for more? Keep reading! The other tips this week will provide further thoughts on this topic.

HOW-TO TIPS

✓ Identify three of the most innovative moments in your life. What connects them?

✓ Talk to a friend about a great idea that was killed because the numbers didn't work.

✓ Compare the financial projections of your company's last five major innovations to the actual results.

✓ See how well two successes and two failures answer the preceding list of five questions that I ask entrepreneurs. Do you see anything missing from this list?

Day 16
Calculate Your Idea's Four *P*'s

Central Question	One-Sentence Answer
What is a quick way to estimate my idea's financial potential?	Multiply population, penetration, price, and purchase frequency to gain quick insight into an idea's potential.

Any marketer can quickly rattle off the so-called four *P*'s of marketing (product, price, place, and promotion). Innovators should also be able to quickly recite the four *P*'s (population, penetration, price, and purchase frequency) that capture their idea's potential.[3]

Let's rewind for a second. In mid-2010, I was sitting in a meeting where an innovation team was painstakingly working through a meticulously crafted spreadsheet detailing the growth potential of its idea. Executives trying to look smart

---

3. If you are an avid Anthony blog reader, then you will recognize this day's guidance. Many of the chapters from the book pick up fragments that I've written on my blog or in one of my books. But this blog post was my most read by a wide margin, so this is pretty much a word-for-word replication. And I got to include a shameless plug for my blog! Check it out at http://blogs.hbr.org/anthony.

lobbed in gotcha questions about specific assumptions. Much discussion ensued.

The team had asked me to observe, but not speak, during the meeting. I sat quietly and took some notes. After the meeting was done, I talked to the innovation team leader.

"That was a really good review," she said. "The executives were really involved, and we have deeper buy-in to our plan."

I had a different perspective. "I don't think a single executive could tell you the essence of the idea, or what makes it compelling," I said. "You *survived* the meeting, but you aren't really any closer to convincing executives that they should invest in this idea."

Before the meeting even took place, the team should have had insight into how big their opportunity had to be to matter to executives. People might say that size doesn't matter, but believe me, size matters an awful lot, particularly inside a large company. Then, the meeting should have focused on two specific questions:

1. Which calculation—simple enough to fit on the back of a napkin—would cross the agreed-upon size threshold?

2. What evidence did the team have that suggested the calculation was plausible?

The four *P*'s of innovation help to answer these questions—and provide a great way to do a quick "sanity check" of any idea's financial potential.

For example, a few years ago, I was working with a team at a consumer health-care company. The team members knew that their idea had to have the potential to cross $100 million in annual gross revenue to get support from leadership.

We knew that the population of severe sufferers for this particular condition was about 10 million people. The product the team was thinking about introducing would cost $20 per package. The team's best guess was that the average consumer would purchase five packages a year.

So that's $1 billion if the team penetrated the entire market. That meant that getting 1 million people—10 percent of the market—would allow the team to cross the magic $100 million mark. That's the four *P*'s in action. Getting to $100 million in revenue required *penetrating* 10 percent of a 10 million *population* who *purchased* the product five times a year at a *price* of $20 per purchase.

Two pieces of advice. First, try to be as precise as you can about your target population. It's easy to fall into the trap of defining the market so broadly that any threshold is achievable ("If we just got $1 from everyone in India . . ."). Create as *small* a market as possible, notably, the people who would constitute your dream customers. Second, don't assert a penetration rate—solve for it after you've estimated the population, pricing, and purchase frequency.

This deceptively simple calculation neatly captures many of the elements of an idea's business model. Does the idea target a niche or a mass population? Is it an occasional or frequent purchase? What channel would support the target price point? What kind of post-sales service would be necessary, given the purchase frequency?

Once you calculate the four *P*'s (and of course, if you add in a fifth—profit margin—you can look at profits instead of revenue), the focus shifts to the second question above: finding systematic ways to determine whether the assumptions behind the calculation have any hope of being true.

For example, our consumer health-care team looked at analogous product introductions and saw that 10 percent was not an unreasonable penetration estimate. Its market research supported a $20 price point. The simple approach built collective confidence in the team's idea.

The deep thinking that goes into creating complicated spreadsheets for ideas can be very useful. But it also can be a way to mistake motion for progress. Make sure you can answer the simple questions before you worry about the complicated ones.

HOW-TO TIPS

✓ Estimate the four *P*'s for a product you used today.

✓ Calculate the four *P*'s for your company's flagship offering.

Day 17
Reverse-Engineer Success

Central Question	One-Sentence Answer
How can I identify an idea's most critical assumptions?	Determine what success looks like, and then identify the two most critical things that would have to happen for success to be obtainable.

The hard part isn't imagining success. It is achieving it.

This was the thought that went through my head as I looked at the one-page summary I had put together. It was February 2010. Earlier that month, I had begun to sketch out the idea for Innosight Labs, our idea to offer business-building services to large corporations (day 3's training described Innosight Labs).

My colleagues generally expressed enthusiasm about the concept and supported taking it forward. They asked me what they thought would be a hard question: "What could this look like in five years?"

Answering that question was actually pretty easy. In a few years, the business would be monumentally successful and we'd be having all sorts of impact with all sorts of interesting companies. The idea fit day 15's pattern, and day 16's four *P*'s calculation looked solid. So, the real question was—what next? What could I do as an intrapreneur (like an entrepreneur but inside a company) to start bridging the massive gulf between an idea detailed in a PowerPoint slide and an impossible-to-disagree-with vision?

It's easy to fall into two traps at this stage. One is to get paralyzed and to keep looking at—and iterating—your PowerPoint slides. Remember—patterns guide, actions decide. Shuffling slide decks wouldn't teach me much. And this wasn't like an image where if you stared long enough, a 3-D picture would emerge.[4]

The other trap is to go to the other extreme and start to run fast in a million directions. That approach clouds learning and makes it difficult to make meaningful progress on an idea.

Some people play certain songs to get inspiration. Me? I turn to the intellectual stylings of McGrath and Cook.

As mentioned in chapter 2, innovation master Rita McGrath (and her esteemed colleague Ian MacMillan) has a very useful way to break apart an idea. It essentially starts with defining success. What outcome would make you happy? Then reverse-engineer that outcome to identify things that would have to be true for success to be attainable. Remember day 14's training ("bring it together"), and look at the idea from multiple perspectives. The goal is to generate a list of assumptions—stated and unstated factors that lie behind success. McGrath and MacMillan provide a wide range of tools to

---

4. You know, I never once have managed to actually see the image.

help with this discovery-driven planning process, from conceptual frameworks to spreadsheet templates.

Of course, the result of this kind of exercise can be overwhelming. You can have dozens, if not hundreds, of assumptions underpinning success. It's easy again to freeze. Enter Scott Cook.

When my colleagues and I were talking to Cook as part of Innosight's work with Procter & Gamble (Cook is on P&G's board), he told us, "For any disruptive team at any one time, there are only maybe two questions they should be focused on. Once they get those two answered or those two hypotheses proven or disproven or altered, then there might be only one or two more in the next stage."

Identifying the two questions that a team should focus on is a mix of art and science. When I am working on an idea, I focus on the five-element checklist detailed in day 15's training (an important problem, a disruptive solution, a viable economic model, the right team, and a clear path to profitability). Then I hold conversations with smart people and use a bit of intuition and judgment to identify *deal killers*, assumptions that, if proven false, would force me to radically rethink my idea. Near-term activities then focus on learning as much about those deal killers as quickly as possible.

For Innosight Labs, two key questions emerged:

1. Was there demand for the service? If the answer was no, it wasn't worth investing.

2. Could we integrate business-building services into our current offering? If the answer was no, we would

have to create a standalone company to offer the service, which we did not want to do.

There were a bunch of other questions to answer (what would we have to build versus borrow? how should the business be led? and so on), but if we could address these two questions in the next ninety days, we would have a good sense of how to take the opportunity forward.

So what did we do? We found two lead clients for which we could conduct focused experiments. The enthusiasm of those clients provided a positive answer to the first question; the success of our integrated delivery model that blended our "traditional" consulting offering with twists to make the output more tangible knocked off the second one. We formally introduced the offering in early 2011.

This technique—imagining success, working backward to understand what would have to be true for success to be plausible, and pinpointing the most critical issues (the deal killers)—is a generally useful approach. We used a variant of it when we were deciding in 2008 whether to shift our *Strategy & Innovation* publication from a printed newsletter to an online model.

We knew that publishing a high-priced bimonthly printed newsletter that had holes in the margins for readers to place it in a three-ring binder just wasn't right. We needed something simpler and more widely available. But we worried that subscribers who paid relatively steep prices for the newsletter might rebel if we shifted to freely distributed online publication. We were prepared to offer them goods and services to compensate them, but didn't want to part with the most precious commodity in a young company—cash!

So we reversed the problem. We identified the maximum amount we were willing to lose in the transition. We calculated the rate at which subscribers would have to demand refunds before we hit that threshold. We simultaneously looked for comparable figures from other publications that had made similar shifts. The simple exercise increased our confidence that any downside risk was manageable, so we proceeded with the shift.[5]

The approach has crept into my personal life as well. When we had made the decision to move to Singapore, my wife and I sat down and said, "What would constitute a great first week in Singapore?" We then worked backward to identify the critical activities that would make the transition as seamless as possible. We had certain assumptions about long-lead-time items, so we addressed them early (lining up movers, developing a perspective on schools for our son, selling our cars) so that we could avoid the last-minute scramble.[6] Using day 9's training, we drew on diverse sets of inputs, such as online guides about living in Singapore and first-person perspectives from other expats. We didn't get everything right, but reverse-engineering success certainly helped us.

---

5. It turned out that almost no one asked for a refund.

6. In fact, both of us found that the last few weeks in Boston were among the most pleasant of our ten years in the city. At least part of the reason for this is that my wife is just insanely organized.

If you ever feel frozen, try to break apart the problem and seek simple, actionable steps to start a journey that can make the impossible possible. Remember, too, that this isn't a one-time exercise. You should constantly be assessing what you know and don't know, to make sure you are focused on the most important things.

HOW-TO TIPS

✓ Look at something you did that didn't work out. What assumption did you make that proved false?

✓ Talk to a friend who is thinking about starting a business. Work with him or her to identify the two most critical questions to answer. Do the same thing on something you are working on.

✓ Go to TechCrunch.com, and read a story about a hot start-up. Write down two questions you would be worried about if you were the CEO.

Day 18
Test Critical Assumptions

Central Question	One-Sentence Answer
How can I learn more about my idea?	Tests are the best ways to learn about existing critical assumptions and to identify new ones.

The plan looked great on paper (plans have a way of doing this). Our team at Innosight was going to create a new business to attack the "missing middle" in the Indian men's grooming market.[7] A single visit to India showed me the promise of this opportunity. If you wanted a shave or haircut, you could go to a high-end salon at a six-star hotel and have a truly world-class experience. Or, you could get incredibly affordable service from the barber whose "salon" was a single chair that sat alongside the road. His instruments at least looked not-too-unhygienic. But if you wanted something in between—a solid experience at a reasonable price—you were pretty much out of luck.

We called our idea Razor Rave. The plan involved an innovative retail store format that essentially put a single

---

7. For curious readers, Innosight does in fact go beyond providing innovation advice. Over the past few years we have incubated or invested in about a dozen businesses in our "Innosight Ventures" unit.

barber chair inside a small pod. Sound familiar? The idea was borrowed liberally from QB House, the simple haircut solution described in day 10's training. The pod's small footprint provided low overheads and high degrees of flexibility. We would use world-class products and envisioned tie-ups with the Gillettes and L'Oréals of the world.

Razor Rave's market research vehicle

Photo by Vijay Raju

Remember, research is valuable, but research has its limits. You can only truly know whether you are right or wrong through action. Good innovators are always on the lookout for ways to run tests—informed, of course, by their research—that can turn assumptions into knowledge.

So would consumers be interested in Razor Rave? There was only one way to find out. We rented a truck and created a salon on wheels by putting a barber's chair on the back of the truck. We drove the truck around the streets of Bangalore for a couple of weeks. High levels of consumer interest told us that the market was ready for to pay price premiums over the roadside barber or local low-end salons. Total cost of learning? About $3,000. We were off!

Then, we discovered what we ended up dubbing the "hero barber" problem. We had launched a few pods on the streets of Bangalore to try to figure out if we really could make the business model work. We quickly found that having a good barber was absolutely critical to draw enough customers to even dream of hitting our financial forecasts. A good barber already had a loyal group of customers who would go out of their way to frequent the Razor Rave pod. These barbers were able to take new customers who wandered in, intrigued by the pod's format, and turn them into repeat customers.

The hair cutters were, in fact, too good. You see, the single-chair format clearly made the barber a hero. Once the barber figured out how critical he was to the success of the business model, the demands started coming. We were left with the unappealing choice of increasing the barber's wages to the point where our economic model began to fall apart, or suffer high attrition. We couldn't find an obvious way out of this quandary without completely redoing the business model, so we decided that it was closing time for Razor Rave.

This story demonstrates an important principle. When you are doing something new, you often don't know the most important assumptions you are making until you put the whole system together. Understanding the subtlety of the hero barber problem—we needed to "hero" the barber to make the business work, but the second we made the barber a hero, the business didn't work—required what academics would call an *integrated experiment*. As my colleagues Matt Eyring and Clark Gilbert noted in a 2010 *Harvard Business Review* article, "These are designed to test how various elements—the actual business model and operations—work together. In essence, they involve launching the business, or some part of it, in miniature."

It sounds a bit daunting, but it doesn't have to be. A detailed spreadsheet that estimates the income statement, balance sheet, and cash flows for a new idea is a form of an integrated experiment, because it shows how the entire business functions. Simple models or simulations can also help to identify what might happen when parts of a system come together. An integrated experiment doesn't have to produce huge results. The point is to learn about the "unknown unknowns"—or the things you didn't know you didn't know.

Integrated experiments contrast with targeted experiments, where you isolate a specific variable and test it. Targeted experiments work well when there is a clear, identified risk that can be tested directly.

For example, a couple of years ago, we were helping a team at Turner Broadcasting System, Inc. (whose cable channels include CNN, TBS, TNT, and the Cartoon Network). The team had an idea for an interesting advertising model. Studies showed that advertisements that had some kind of contextual meaning resonated with consumers. For example, when you search for something on Google, the connection of advertisements to specific search terms makes the ads more memorable. The team wondered whether it couldn't bring a similar model to television. To illustrate the idea, the project leader showed people a scene in a popular movie with a high-speed car chase. The action stopped, and the first commercial was for BMW's latest car. Memorable, isn't it?

One of the critical questions was whether Turner Broadcasting's programming had enough identifiable points of context to support a widespread program. The team designed a clever test. It gave a group of summer interns two weeks and asked them to identify points of context that might be of interest to a select group of advertisers in a handful of movies and television shows to which Turner Broadcasting had rights. Not only did the interns find plenty of points of context, but the results of this focused experiment ended up forming a vital part of the pitch Turner Broadcasting made to advertisers for the offering it dubbed TVinContext.

Thomas Edison appeared on the Mount Rushmore of Innovation for his quip "Genius is 1 percent inspiration and 99 percent perspiration." If you (or those summer interns) aren't sweating, you aren't innovating. Whenever you have an idea, try to think about the quickest way to learn about critical assumptions—or to find out the critical assumption you *didn't* realize you were making.

HOW-TO TIPS

✓ List the five biggest assumptions behind your idea; design and execute ways to learn more about those assumptions without spending any money.

✓ Identify a way to learn more about an idea in sixty minutes or less. Execute it! See my blog at http://blogs.hbr.org/anthony/2011/03/60_minutes_to_a_more_innovativ.html for some ideas.

✓ Think about a recent life change. What advice would you give yourself before the change? What could you have done to learn more about "unknown unknowns"?

Day 19
Bring Ideas to Life

Central Question	One-Sentence Answer
How can I get people behind my idea?	Find creative ways to bring ideas to life in order to build buy-in and motivate action.

Testing sounds a bit academic, but it shouldn't be. Look carefully at the examples in the previous pages. Align sold its product to consumers online. Razor Rave ran tests to see if it could get people to come inside the shaving truck. Turner Broadcasting pitched its ideas to advertisers. Selling—and developing the right collateral to support the sales process— is a critical skill for any innovator.

In fact, a good innovator is always in sales mode. In the course of a day, an innovator could have to accomplish many typical sales tasks:

- Convince customers to buy something they have never bought before.

- Get skeptical senior management to invest in doing something different.

FIGURE 7-1

- Pry money out of the hands of tight-fisted venture capitalists.

- Urge friends or coworkers to join an underfunded business that statistics suggest is going to fail.

- Cajole a reticent department to free up a resource.

- Push a team to continue forward when bad news inevitably strikes.

Selling is a great way to test an idea's most critical assumptions. And it is very hard to sell something without bringing the idea to life in some way. Just try to get people excited about a dense PowerPoint presentation populated with facts and figures. It's next to impossible. For example, figure 7-1 shows screenshots from a pitch for an idea we developed for a consumer electronics company. Do you think this kind of pitch resonated more than PowerPoint slides?

Start instead by developing a simple way to capture the essence of your idea. Remember the Hollywood pitch described in Chapter 1? The approach crystallizes an idea into an anchor analogy (what is it similar to) and a twist (what makes it unique). I've found that ideas that lack a good Hollywood pitch are often hard to communicate to customers and stakeholders. While a good Hollywood pitch doesn't mean the idea is any good, it at least means that people can quickly understand it.

People like to see and touch things. Beyond Hollywood pitches, we've used the following to help bring ideas to life in our efforts:

- Ninety-second videos

- Mock magazine advertisements describing the envisioned product or service with a semiclever tagline (believe it or not, thinking of a tagline helps to bring great clarity around an idea)

- *MacGyver*-type prototypes (a prototype held together by real or virtual duct tape)[8]

- Storyboards that present a multiframe visual (like a cartoon) depicting how a customer would experience a product or service

---

8. In my travels in Asia, I have found that *MacGyver* is a surprisingly well-understood cultural reference. For those who don't know it, *MacGyver* was a television show in the 1980s and 1990s whose eponymous protagonist had a stunning ability to use a Swiss Army knife, duct tape, and readily available materials to create contraptions that saved him from certain death.

- Skits depicting television advertisements

- Semifunctional Web sites created using free services like Wix.com

- A newspaper article five years in the future profiling the transformational impact of an idea

These suggestions may look a bit intimidating, but they are surprisingly accessible. For example, my ten-year-old niece created a pretty slick video using a freely accessible tool. The goal isn't to produce something that looks like it was done by a professional. Rather, the goal is to ensure that you have really considered the essence of your idea and to help yourself to communicate it more clearly than a detailed PowerPoint slide ever could. As an added bonus, every person I have seen follow one of these approaches has learned more about his or her own idea. After all, you also have to sell to yourself whatever it is that you are making or doing!

The other trick is to have other people do the pitching for you. This could involve having a customer come to an important meeting to describe how he or she feels about your idea, or showing a video testimonial. Even the most analytically minded people react strongly to hearing a real person give a personal reaction to an idea.

If you do feel compelled to do PowerPoint, at least follow Guy Kawasaki's 10/20/30 rule—ten PowerPoint slides, designed to be discussed in twenty minutes, with no smaller than 30-point font. But with the tools at our disposal today, a

PowerPoint presentation should really be a last resort. Do your homework, of course, but don't bore people to death with it.

HOW-TO TIPS

- ✓ Watch an online video of someone you consider an excellent salesperson. Write down the three things this person does to accentuate a pitch.

- ✓ Write down a one-sentence slogan that you would put on a magazine advertisement for your idea.

- ✓ Spend five minutes pitching a concept from a chapter in this book to a friend.

- ✓ Watch a TED video, and analyze why TED speakers are so effective at selling an idea—at changing their listener's view between the beginning and the end of a talk.

Day 20
Embrace Everyday Experimentation

Central Question	One-Sentence Answer
How can I get good at experimentation?	Be on constant lookout for ways to run everyday experiments.

Coming up with and executing the kinds of activities described in the past few days' training might feel a bit daunting. It doesn't have to be if you make experimentation part of your everyday routine.

Many iconic innovators are portrayed as highly experimental. Innovation master Thomas Edison was famous for being a fiddler and a tinkerer. British entrepreneur and Virgin Group chairman Sir Richard Branson never met anything he wouldn't try at least once. Experimentation is a very healthy thing. Not only does it get you to try different things, but it also prepares you for those sudden shifts that increasingly seem to characterize our lives.

Sometimes the notion of experimentation scares people, because it sounds like the sort of thing that requires specialized equipment, knowledge, and funding. It doesn't. Some of the best experiments can take place in your head. Just as chess players quickly visualize several moves ahead when determining their move, innovators conduct thought experiments to figure out an idea's potential. Mark Johnson shares a great example of a thought experiment in *Seizing the White Space*. He describes how the chemical company Dow Corning was thinking about rolling out a new low-cost Web site to distribute its products (day 24 discusses this idea in more depth). Historically, Dow Corning relied on its salaried sales force to sell products to customers. The innovation team did a thought experiment to project what would happen if Dow Corning launched its Web site within the mainstream organization. Johnson explains the result: "The new model got crushed. It was too foreign to Dow Corning's current modes of working. The way forward became clear. The new venture would need to be free from the core business model if it was going to thrive."

One of the best ways to get good at experimentation is to find ways to embed it into every day activities. Here's a personal example.

I was in a hotel.[9] I woke up and started looking around for the coffee maker. After all, for years my day had started with a hot cup. Like all habits, this one didn't take much thought. It was just what I did in the morning. It was an easy habit to maintain because seemingly every hotel has a small coffee maker in it.

---

9. Don't worry, the story doesn't end with me in a bathtub missing my kidneys.

Except that this hotel room, for whatever reason, had no coffee. I had a few things to do, so I couldn't go downstairs and grab a cup of coffee. It wasn't that big a deal, because surely, there would be coffee at the meeting I was attending. But there was none in sight. I figured I was set up for a disastrous day, but I actually found myself functioning better in the morning when there was a longer gap between waking up and having coffee.

It could have been a random occurrence tied to the specifics of the circumstance, so I began to experiment more consciously. One day, I'd wake up, work for a bit, have a cup of coffee with breakfast, then shower. The next day, I would wake up, immediately have a shower, have breakfast, go to work, and have a cup later in the morning. These weren't perfectly controlled experiments, but I did begin to notice that I tended to function best when there was some kind of space between waking up and ingesting caffeine.

Think about all the small experiments you could run in a day. Change how you commute to work. Alter the order of the things you do in the day. Eat five small meals instead of three large ones. Don't shave one morning. The avenues for experimentation explode in the office. Shut your BlackBerry off until 10 a.m. Start the day by logging into Facebook instead of e-mail (or e-mail instead of Facebook if you are under thirty-five). Commit to being the last person to speak in a meeting. Introduce your comments first.

Karl Ronn, the former P&G leader who described the importance of being close to context in research in day 6's training, also believes in being close to context in experimentation: "Always try the experiments yourself. If you want someone to do it, you have to at least imagine trying it yourself and find out what surprised or confused you. This is the empathy that is needed."

Once you start to think about experimentation, it is hard to stop. You will begin to see dozens of daily tasks for which experimentation might show you a better way.

Think back to high school science class to get the most out of experimentation. Document your hypothesis. "If I make a left on Beacon Street, I will shave four minutes off my commute." "I can avoid the 3 p.m. energy lull if I have fruit at 2 p.m." "I will finish editing that report if I turn off e-mail for an hour." Then, of course, check the results with what you hypothesized.

Experimentation need not be expensive or time-consuming. One of the most common questions from people inside companies is, "What do I do if I can't get my management to give me a larger budget or more staff?" Of course, you can beg, plead, or pout. Or you can prove it. Find some kind of way to scrape together low- or no-cost experiments that address management's most critical assumptions. Show management what you learned without resources. It makes quite a compelling argument for what you could do with a bit more resources.

HOW-TO TIPS

✓ Identify three everyday routines that could be grounds for experimentation.

✓ Look at a looming life decision. Identify two options. Ask what would have to be true for you to choose option two. Identify an experiment that could give you more information.

✓ Take an idea that you have. Identify three costless ways to learn more about the idea's potential.

Day 21
Savor Surprises

Central Question	One-Sentence Answer
How can I learn the right things from my experiments?	Experience the raw data, and focus on the findings you did not expect.

This week's training has been all about assessing and testing an idea. Of course, you aren't doing this for fun. You are trying to gain confidence that you are moving in the right direction—or get critical learning that helps you change your idea in ways that increase the odds of success (this is what innovation master Steve Blank would call *pivoting*).

Remember that innovation is an iterative process. You might go back to day 14 and reframe your plan. Or you might hop back to day 3 to rethink the job you identified as needing to be done. Or perhaps you will turn to day 17 and identify two new questions to answer. Before you do any of these things, you need to make sure you have learned the right things from your tests.

Unfortunately, extracting that learning isn't easy, largely because of a factor that psychologists call *confirmation bias*. In everyday terms, it means that people see what they want to see. If you have a belief, you see the things that conform to that belief, and you ignore the things that don't. Confirmation bias explains why two people can look at the same data and see completely different things.

One of the great examples of confirmation bias at work comes from a 1954 study by Albert Hartorf and Hadley Cantril. The researchers showed students from Dartmouth and Princeton a filmstrip of a controversial football game between the two teams. Perhaps not surprisingly, the two groups saw the game very differently. Princeton viewers thought that the Dartmouth squad had committed more than twice as many violations as had Princeton's team. Dartmouth students thought the two teams had committed an equal number of violations. Neutral observers thought Dartmouth had committed more fouls, but nowhere near the number that Princeton students reported. As the great philosopher Paul Simon said, "Still a man hears what he wants to hear and disregards the rest."[10]

Innovators who are testing their ideas need to be very aware of confirmation bias. Think about the old parable about the two shoe salespeople who go to a market where the locals don't wear shoes. One seller sends a note to the head office: "No one wears shoes here; returning home." The

---

10. That's from the song "The Boxer." Great thanks to Robert I. Sutton, who quotes Simon in *Good Boss, Bad Boss: How to Be the Best . . . and Learn from the Worst* (New York: Business Plus, 2010). Sutton also quotes a study that shows how National Basketball Association teams will keep playing players who were drafted early even if objective statistics in professional contests suggest that they are duds. As a Washington Wizards fan, I would call this the *Kwame Brown phenomenon.*

other salesperson sends a note saying: "The market is wide open! Please send more shoes."

Where you stand indeed depends on where you sit.

I saw an example of confirmation bias up close while working with a leading consumer packaged-goods brand. We'll disguise the story by calling the company Gargantuan, Inc., and pretend that the company makes a delicious breakfast cereal. The company had long prided itself on its technical expertise. While competitors mostly fought battles of marketing, Gargantuan had legions of scientists working on improving the measurable quality of its product. Over the years, Gargantuan increased the space between it and its leading competitors and obtained dominant market share. Its cereal was crunchier than its leading competitor, Simpleton, by 30 percent; had 20 percent more nutrients; and tasted 15 percent better. Obtaining this quality required that consumers use a low-cost bowl affixed to their kitchen counter that worked seamlessly with Gargantuan's cereal to produce the end benefit. Since everyone eats in the kitchen and the bowl was simple and inexpensive, no one complained about this solution.

Then, in the mid-1990s, Simpleton introduced a very different solution. It put its cereal in a bar that allowed consumers to eat it on the go. Simpleton intentionally sacrificed quality in pursuit of convenience. Gargantuan's scientists found that the gap in crunchiness, nutrients, and taste increased to 40, 30, and 25 percent, respectively.

Those findings came from a carefully constructed piece of research Gargantuan commissioned to understand

Simpleton's new solution. The large company also asked consumers which solution they preferred. The answer? A majority of consumers stated that they preferred Simpleton's solution.

This puzzled the scientists. "But consumers report that we are better along every measurable dimension," the scientists said. "How could they prefer Simpleton?"

Of course, one explanation (the right one) was that while Gargantuan rated better along those traditional dimensions, more and more consumers sought convenience. But that's not the way the industry traditionally worked. So the Gargantuan scientists concluded that they *must have asked the question the wrong way*. They rewrote the survey, running a series of pretests to make sure that survey takers understood the intent of each question. They didn't change the essence of any of the questions; they didn't start working on a competitive response to Simpleton's fast-growing offering. They ran the survey, and waited for the result to come back.

The results didn't change a bit. Consumers still reported that Gargantuan's offering was better; they still reported preferring Simpleton's offering. Punishingly, the six months Gargantuan spent fine-tuning its research instrument gave Simpleton time to introduce a new and improved version of its convenience-based product, putting Gargantuan even further behind.

Scott Cook (three mentions in week 3!) guides people to savor surprises. That is, instead of looking for data that fits your hypothesis, specifically study the data you *didn't* expect to get. Scientists would call this studying the anomalies, and it is in those anomalies where the great insight often lies. After all, if an experiment showed you what you expected, you didn't need to run the experiment.

How do you avoid confirmation bias and more successfully savor surprises? Consider these three tricks. First, don't separate researchers and decision makers. If there is separation, researchers will feel an overwhelming need to summarize their market research in easy-to-digest sound bites. That means throwing away outliers and anomalies. If decision makers experience the raw data, they can spot signals that third-party researchers might miss. When we are working with companies to pilot new businesses, we insist on conducting any consumer-facing work ourselves so that we can pounce on these signals and make adjustments as we learn new information.

The second trick is to frame things as a reverse of what you are truly expecting. I tell teams that their initial hypothesis when investigating whether to advise clients to invest in a new-growth business should always be "We should *not* invest in this new-growth business." That means they carefully study the results that fit that hypothesis, and, of course, carefully study the "outliers" as well.

Finally, involve people who don't have "skin in the game" in the discussion. Thought leaders who describe the wisdom of crowds note that groups outperform experts because while *individuals* suffer from confirmation bias, a *group* does not (individual biases essentially cancel out, except, of course, when manias, bubbles, and herd behavior take over). Even the injection of one outside voice can help you savor surprises.

You are probably wondering what happened to Gargantuan, right? Well, the company got its act together. After losing significant market share for a couple of years, it introduced a product that successfully stopped Simpleton in its tracks. And it started work on an innovative product that would eliminate the need for breakfast altogether.[11]

HOW-TO TIPS

✓ Identify a contrarian friend who can help you avoid confirmation bias.

✓ Read detailed qualitative comments from a recent market research report.

✓ Look at outlying data that was discarded from a management presentation to identify gems worth savoring.

---

11. Tantalizing, isn't it? I'm still not telling what category this is really about. Ask me in 2013.

Week 3 Wrap-Up

The focus of week 3 was assessing and testing your innovative idea. You hopefully answered four questions this week:

1. How confident am I about my idea's potential?

2. What are the most critical assumptions?

3. How can I design experiments to learn about those assumptions?

4. What do the experiment's results suggest about my idea's potential?

More broadly, remember three phrases.

1. Deal killers: Assumptions that, if proven false, mean your current strategy is not viable.

2. Discovery-driven planning: An approach that involves imagining success, determining what would need to be true for success to be achievable, and executing tests around critical assumptions.

3. Test and learn: No matter how smart you are, your first plan is sure to be wrong—test and learn to figure out *how*.

WEEK 4

MOVING FORWARD

If you have dutifully done everything in the past few weeks, you have, hopefully, developed a robust idea that has been through early testing. This week's training details what comes next. First, days 22–24 describe how to apply your effort in ways that will maximize your chances of success. Days 25 and 26 particularly focus on challenges facing corporate readers. Days 27 and 28 finish the innovation program by showing you how to ensure that progress continues beyond these twenty-eight days.

Specifically, this week will help you to:

1. Manage resources in a way that helps you maximize progress

2. Determine what you should do yourself and what others can do

3. Develop mechanisms to guard against the sucking sound of the core

4. Create a training program to improve your innovation capabilities

Day 22
Embrace Selective Scarcity

Central Question	One-Sentence Answer
How much should I invest in innovation?	Embrace selective scarcity with tight timelines, single decision makers, and constrained strategic choices.

Here's a quick question—why didn't former Apple CEO Steve Jobs come from sub-Saharan Africa? Thinking about that question leads to an interesting discussion about scarcity, abundance, and innovation.

There is a general viewpoint that constraints and innovation tend to be friends. Plato, after all, said something that morphed into the aphorism "Necessity is the mother of innovation." Heck, one of the core themes in my last book (*The Silver Lining*) was that constraints imposed by a downturn would help innovation: "Tough economic times are going to force innovators to do what they should have been doing already."

It's close to perceived wisdom that abundance can weigh down innovation. My former colleague Bradley Gambill and coauthors James Clayton and Douglas Harned wrote an excellent *McKinsey Quarterly* article that summed up this viewpoint nicely with its provocative title, "The Curse of Too Much Capital." The article proposed that corporations would often crush innovation by providing it too much capital.

So back to the question that started today's tip. If constraints unleash innovation and if abundance inhibits it, why didn't Steve Jobs come from sub-Saharan Africa? Why are the most innovative companies in the world resource-rich? Why do the most successful start-ups largely come from the richest countries?

Of course, the answer is that it's pretty hard to develop a new-growth business when you have to spend all day working to make sure you can feed your family. Abundance can certainly run amok—you wouldn't pick someone who is morbidly obese to win a marathon. But scarcity can, too—the marathon prospects of someone starving are pretty poor.

The best way to encourage innovation is to embrace *selective scarcity*, where you place limits on three factors whose abundance can in fact crush innovation.

The first constraint is time. If you accept the premise that the only thing you can be sure of in the early days is that your first strategy is wrong, create a forcing function to stop you from going in the wrong direction for too long. Venture capitalists will interact with early-stage companies on a weekly, if not daily, basis. They are trying to help the entrepreneurs make sense of the latest data they have received and make real-time decisions about their strategy. Thirty- or forty-five-day review windows are fine. Anything longer than that is very, very dangerous because it can lead a team to overthink issues, to analyze when it should be doing, or to make things overly complicated. Strategy can't be scheduled. Setting what seems like absurdly tight deadlines can motivate progress.

The second constraint relates to where you focus. The absolutely worst thing to do is treat innovation like an unbounded exercise. When the answer to the question of "What have you taken off the table?" is "Nothing," nine times out of ten, the effort will go nowhere. Letting chaos reign is a good recipe for . . . chaos. Consider the thought experiment posed by Chip Heath and Dan Heath in the book *Made to Stick*. The brothers Heath suggest spending fifteen seconds writing down all the items you can think of that are white. Good job. Now, spend fifteen seconds writing down all the items that are white and that *can be found in a refrigerator*. If you are like most people, the second, constrained, task was much easier than the first, unconstrained one. Be very clear about the definition of success and acceptable and unacceptable tactics. Make sure the unacceptable list is longer than the acceptable one. You might think that you are shackling innovation, but in reality you are enabling it—and being honest about things that will ultimately get in the way of success. Innosight uses a tool called *goals and bounds* to help innovators clarify what specific options they are taking off the table.

Both of these constraints—time and narrower focus—are meaningful whether you are on your own or in a large organization. The last constraint—the number of decision makers—is specific to people working inside corporations.

Innovation is not done best by committee, because it's almost always easier to find flaws in an idea than to see its beauty. Almost every project I've seen that has multiple stakeholders ends up like many things that make it through most legislative processes. It's acceptable to everyone and delightful to no one. As the old saying goes, "A camel is a horse designed by committee." Of course, many companies will say that they have a sole decision maker for an effort, but that's rarely the case. Just about everyone who is senior in an organization is used to having suggestions acted upon, and quickly. And just about every midlevel employee is used to jumping when someone up the chain makes an offhand comment. It requires fierce discipline to be clear that there is one, and only one, voice that truly matters for a project. And sometimes that voice could be different from the person with the "biggest title."

There are other areas where abundance is less troublesome. If you are tight enough about time, financial resources take care of themselves. It's hard to blow too much money in tight windows, and careful oversight from a single decision maker helps to make sure that nothing too wacky takes place. And it is actually pretty bizarre for big companies to be too frugal with their innovation spending. After all, one of their key sources of competitive advantage is a core business that provides sufficient capital to reinvest in innovation. Those resources coupled with unique market knowledge should enable corporations to do what entrepreneurs cannot.

I once had a problem with large teams, because I've seen too many large teams get caught chasing their own tail (there's even a wonderful phrase to describe this—*Penrosian slack*). I've come to the conclusion, however, that the root cause of the chase-your-tail phenomenon is a lack of clarity about whose voice really matters. If your team has five people who all answer different masters, you have a recipe for swirl. If you have fifty people who have a clear view of whose voice matters and whose voice can be ignored, you will get the benefits of extra arms and legs without the swirl.

Selective scarcity (or careful constraints) can enable innovation. Going overboard can cripple it.

HOW-TO TIPS

✓ Give yourself a twenty-four-hour deadline on a task to see what happens with forced focus.

✓ Identify the most successful innovation efforts in your company over the past few years.[1] What did they have in abundance? What was scarce?

✓ Create a list of activities on which you or your team is currently working. Identify the decision maker for each activity. Once you get past five decision makers, admit you have a problem that needs to be addressed.

---

1. You may note that many how-to tips draw from analyzing successful and failed innovation efforts. As a rule, companies should conduct after-action reviews to capture what worked and what didn't work for a particular effort.

Day 23
Amplify Your Resources

Central Question	One-Sentence Answer
Where can I find resources for innovation?	Leverage external resources, and redirect currently committed resources.

While day 22 emphasized embracing selective scarcity, you of course need *some* resources to drive innovation efforts. That was the intention behind a question I received from a workshop attendee in the Philippines: "All this sounds great, but we don't have enough resources to pull this off. What should we do?"

It is a common, and important, question. I was feeling in a pop culture mood that day, so my answer was "*Under the Dome*, *Zombieland*, and *Honey, I Shrunk the Kids*."

Even though Filipino audiences generally are attuned to U.S. culture, that response drew some blank stares. I went on to explain.

Under the Dome is a 2009 book by noted horror author Stephen King. The book describes the impact caused by a dome's sudden appearance over Chester's Mill, a fictional town in Maine.[2] The dome lets in enough air to let people live, but blocks out everything else.

People too frequently approach innovation like the residents of Chester's Mill. That is, they feel as if they have to do everything themselves. But the best innovators are constantly looking to connect with outside resources. Break free of the dome, and find outsiders who are keenly motivated to help you.

For example, consider Howard M. Stevenson and Jose-Carlos Jarillo Mossi's "R&R," the quirky Harvard Business School case study that has opened the Entrepreneurial Management class at the Harvard Business School for years. Where most HBS cases are open-ended, with the protagonist ending the case looking out the window and pondering some tough decision, the authors describe how an entrepreneur named Bob Reiss seized an opportunity he saw in the toy industry.

In the early 1980s, Reiss saw that the board game Trivial Pursuit was catching on in Canada. His industry experience (he had previously worked in the toy industry) told him that there was an opportunity to introduce a similar style of game in the United States. He worked with a slew of partners to quickly introduce a *TV Guide* board game.[3] If you review

---

2. The plot bears some striking similarities to *The Simpsons* movie, which was released in 2007. King apparently started working on his novel in the late 1970s, however.

3. To my younger readers: *TV Guide* used to be a powerhouse media brand, with weekly circulation at its peak of close to 20 million. That isn't a typo. Of course, the Internet changed that.

the case and break out your calculator, you will see that Reiss turned an investment of about $50,000 of his own money into a cool $2.2 million in about twelve months.

The case is a great workshop tool, because a good fifteen-minute discussion unearths a simple but powerful point about the relationship between risk and innovation. I will ask people, "So what did Reiss do?" Usually at least one attendee will say, "He didn't do anything! His partners did all the work." And that's the point. Reiss found the best people in the world to handle particular parts of his business. People often think that entrepreneurs consciously seek out risk. Most don't. Rather, they smartly *manage* risk.

Sometimes innovators seem to think they get extra credit for doing things themselves. In fact, the best innovators have a degree of humility in that they recognize their own limitations. They implicitly follow the philosophy of Chris Killingstad, the CEO of Tennant, a $500 million cleaning solutions company. Killingstad tells his company to "do what we do best, and partner for the rest."

The resources at your disposal need not end at your floor, building, or (if you are in a large company) department. The world can literally be your oyster, if you look at it in the right way.

Breaking free of the dome can help you extend your resources. The next two references help you make sure you focus your resources in the right way.

Zombieland was a gory but enjoyable 2009 movie starring Jesse Eisenerg, Woody Harrelson, Emma Stone, and Abigail Breslin—and a great cameo by Bill Murray. My point when I mentioned this movie to the Filipino audience had nothing to do with the movie's plot, but did reference zombies, the walking undead.[4] If you look closely enough at the way most companies approach innovation, you see a surprisingly high number of *zombie projects*. That is, projects with little hope—some of which have even been officially shut down—that linger on. Individuals suffer from the zombie project problem as well. Ask how many items on your to-do list really matter. Time management experts suggest that you probably are working on too many things that seem urgent but really aren't that important. So start by cutting the roughly 30 percent of things that are shuffling zombies.

If you are a senior leader in a large corporation, you have to look for zombie divisions or product lines, too. Innovation master Richard Foster's research shows that companies that outperform the market are good not just at creating new businesses, but in shutting down or spinning off old businesses. For example, in the early 1980s, Procter & Gamble was an unsexy provider of consumer staples. Thirty years later, it had powerhouse beauty product lines like Olay, Pantene, Wella, and Cover Girl, and a multibillion-dollar fine fragrances line that managed perfumes for high fashion brands like Hugo Boss and Dolce & Gabbana. That transformation involved a healthy dose of creation, but it also involved selling off or shutting down long-term standouts like Jif peanut butter, Pringles

---

4. Most zombie movies are references to the pernicious impact that the pale glow of television has on society. My favorite zombie book: Max Brooks, *World War Z: An Oral History of the Zombie War* (New York: Crown, 2006). My favorite zombie movie: *28 Days Later*.

potato chips, Crisco food shortening, Folgers coffee, and Spic and Span household cleaners.

Honey, I Shrunk the Kids sticks in my memory mostly because I had a major crush on Amy O'Neill, who played one of the teenagers inadvertently shrunk by Rick Moranis's scatterbrained scientist. It also serves as an apt metaphor for the second way to find resources for innovation—cut the size of the nonzombie project teams by 30 to 50 percent. Why? Small teams almost always move faster than large teams. Well-oiled teams with a single master can be powerful, but they are the exception. Most companies have overly large project teams.

These efforts to reduce the team size allow you to increase focus and financial resources on high-potential ideas that are getting close to a major inflection point or on new initiatives. You aren't magically creating more resources here—you are just making sure that you get the most of your resources by organizing appropriately.

One place where you shouldn't compromise—having a full-time project leader. It's possible to be a valuable part-time *contributor* to a project. And it's possible to play a vital part-time role in any project that closely conforms to a company's core processes or business model. But part-time business builders don't work. There are simply too many challenges that require constant attention. Remember, most start-up businesses fail, and that's with diligent, minute-by-minute attention from the founding team. Some things just take time and dedicated focus. As the old saying goes, nine women can't make a baby in a month.

All of a sudden, resources don't look like much of a problem, do they? Escape the dome, kill the zombies, and shrink the teams, and you are on your way!

HOW-TO TIPS

- ✓ List all the activities on which you are personally working. Any zombies on the list?

- ✓ Create a list of every innovation project currently under way at your company, including those that aren't on an official plan but take up people's time.

- ✓ Document three things that you are doing yourself that an outside specialist could do quicker, cheaper, or more effectively.

Day 24
Break the Sucking Sound
of the Core

Central Question	One-Sentence Answer
How can I avoid the sucking sound of the core?	Active leadership, new voices, safe spaces, and smart borrowing can help protect innovators from the sucking sound of the core.

One of the most powerful—and most dangerous—management concepts introduced in the last fifty years was contained in "Core Competence of the Corporation," a 1990 *Harvard Business Review* article by Gary Hamel and C. K. Prahalad. The concept is powerful because it has helped hundreds if not thousands of companies become very clear about what they can do that makes them special. It is also very dangerous, because the more a company focuses on what it perceives as its core competence, the more it risks running into what we've termed the "sucking sound of the core."

I put my grandfather on the Mount Rushmore of Innovation to serve as a reminder of the double-entry notion of corporate capabilities. Remember, every corporate capability has a corresponding disability. This is why it is so important to remember innovation master Vijay Govindarajan's advice of forgetting some core capabilities and learning new ones.

The more successful you are, the greater the pull of the core. As a simple analogy, think about learning a new language. When my family and I moved to Singapore, my then four-year-old son started taking immersive Mandarin classes every afternoon for an hour. He quickly picked up the language, because he didn't have to *un*learn complex grammatical rules. It is much harder for me to get his level of proclivity, because I have to work to unwire a lifetime of grammar lessons.[5]

Breaking the sucking sound of the core is hard, but it is possible. One great example is Dow Corning's Xiameter.

I love the example because the story isn't widely known, even though it has appeared in a number of Innosight-authored books (the best detailed example is in *Seizing the White Space*). Further, it provides rich instruction on how to break the sucking sound of the core.

Dow Corning epitomizes the Midwest of the United States. The people are smart, unfailingly polite, and passionate about the production and distribution of silicone-based products. These products are used in thousands of applications, ranging from personal-care products like shampoos to

---

5. Even worse, it seems that languages just aren't one of my areas of strength. I studied Spanish for about fifteen years, and today I can ask, "Can I have a beer, please?" and "Where is the bathroom?" These are useful phrases, no doubt (and one necessitates the other), but pretty poor output from fifteen years of education.

sealants on the space shuttle. Dow Corning is one of three major employers in Midland, Michigan (The Dow Chemical Company and Chemical Bank being the others), and it plays a critical role in the town.

In the early 2000s, Dow Corning identified a threat that keeps many Western executives up at night—the specter of commoditization driven by Chinese competitors. The company saw that it was losing market share in the least demanding tier of its industry. Dow Corning historically competed by having scientists who would work alongside its customers to tailor-make its silicone products for their specific needs. While the firm's large volumes made it the industry's low-cost producer, the overheads involved in its basic model rendered Dow Corning noncompetitive against pure price-based competitors.

To its credit, Dow Corning recognized the threat. It also recognized that responding to the threat would require a combination of organizational and business model innovation. It formed a team under the guidance of then controller Don Sheets. The team's charter was to find a way to flip the commoditization threat into a growth opportunity.

The model Sheets and the team developed involved, in essence, a new sales channel. Instead of having a direct, consultative sales process that required high-cost scientists, customers go to the Xiameter Web site and order chemicals online. Instead of ordering any amount of chemical, customers could only order in bulk. And instead of having complicated price negotiations, Xiameter customers would get market-competitive prices. The business was a massive commercial success for Dow Corning, quickly returning the company's initial capital investment and helping it grow both its low-end and its high-end business.

Reviewing the case history helps to highlight four elements that helped the team ward off the sucking sound of the core:

1. Active senior leadership: Sheets eventually rose up to be Dow Corning's chief financial officer. The project was started by then Dow Corning CEO Gary Anderson. Stephanie Burns, who replaced Anderson in 2004, actively championed the effort.

2. Not the usual suspects: Sheets sought a specific type of team member, one that wouldn't be afraid of doing things differently. He had an interesting approach to recruiting Dow Corning people to the team. When he met a prospect who seemed to have potential, he'd offer the person the job on the spot. Those who took it had the ability to follow the adage of Facebook CEO Mark Zuckerberg: "Move fast and break things."[6]

3. "Safe space": Dow Corning intentionally kept the Xiameter effort largely separate from the core business, which allowed it to "forget" key elements of Dow Corning's core capabilities.

---

6. I'm sure some of you are wondering, "Doesn't that mean Sheets suffered from adverse selection, in that the only people who *could* say yes on the spot probably weren't very good?" Look at it from the other perspective. Perhaps the best people for the job were people who might be floundering in the core business because they were better wired for more innovative endeavors.

4. Smart borrowing from the core: Xiameter had a new logo, sales channel, order flow, and so on. It did utilize the same enterprise planning system that the core business used, because it found that the rules embedded in this system enabled its business. The team followed Govindarajan's advice about borrowing—instead of looking for cost savings, they looked for things that would provide competitive advantage.

The last point bears repeating. Instead of looking for cost savings, they looked for things that would provide competitive advantage. Capabilities are double edged. Every asset has a corresponding liability. And *nothing* is free. Borrowing a core brand means adhering to whatever guidelines exist around that brand. Borrowing the financial tools from the core business means taking whatever implicit assumptions lurk beneath that model.

I've seen the sucking sound of the core derail a number of promising growth ventures. The right leadership actions, however, can let a venture break free and realize its inherent potential.

HOW-TO TIPS

✓ Create a detailed blueprint of what you should borrow and what core capability you absolutely must forget.

✓ Identify two historical efforts that succumbed to the sucking sound of the core and subsequently had less impact than they would have otherwise.

Day 25
Manage the Interfaces

Central Question	One-Sentence Answer
How do I manage interfaces between a new business and the core business?	Use a range of techniques to make sure you don't accidentally remember what you are trying to forget.

The previous three days' tips should have been useful for all readers. The next two days more specifically focus on some of the particular challenges facing large corporations. Hopefully, these tips will prove interesting to individual innovators as well.

The sucking sound of the core is a powerful force. It takes new growth initiatives that look to be set up for success and slowly and surely transforms them into things that bear a striking similarity to the core business. The result is rarely the intended outcome, and it's often disappointing. A great example of this was described in Robert A. Guth's 2009 *Wall Street Journal* article, "Microsoft Bid to Beat Google Builds on a History of Misses," which detailed how Microsoft had all the pieces to create Google—and blew it.

First, a short primer on Google. While many people consider it a technology company, its real magic is its business model. It allows companies to "buy" keywords, so that when an individual searches for a term, he or she sees an advertisement tied to that term. Companies only pay if someone actually clicks on an advertisement. Google has a dynamic system that prices keywords in real time according to demand. This advertising program, called AdWords, has been the driver of Google's ascendancy.

It turns out that Microsoft was working on an eerily similar solution in the early 2000s. There was no individual decision that doomed these efforts. Instead, a series of subtle decisions led to Microsoft's missing the opportunity. For example, Microsoft wanted to test search-based advertising on its MSN portal. But the portal's business leaders worried that the advertisements would draw users away from the banner advertisements that served as a lucrative source of revenue, so they made the search results hard for users to find. Disappointing test results were at least one factor that led Microsoft to deprioritize the opportunity.

Avoiding this pitfall requires thoughtfully managing the interfaces between the core business and the new business. Of course, the simplest answer is to completely spin off the new business and make it a stand-alone entity so there are no interfaces between the core and new businesses. Department store retailer Dayton Hudson followed this approach in the early 1960s, when it set up a separate subsidiary to go after the emerging discount retailing opportunity. That subsidiary—Target—now represents that company's core business. Spinning out a new business indeed gives that business the freedom to follow whatever course it desires, but it also limits the degree to which the new business can benefit from the skills or other assets of the core business.

Beyond spinning out, three mechanisms can help you manage the interface between the core and the new business.

First, create a specific mechanism to manage potential points of tension. For example, back in 2003, Cisco Systems purchased Linksys for $500 million. The express reason why Cisco made the purchase was to get Linksys's business model. Cisco's historical strength was in the enterprise market. Key elements of its historical business model were high investment in research and development (R&D) and a direct sales force. Its gross margins averaged about 70 percent. Linksys had almost no R&D investment and sold to large retailers like Best Buy. Its margins averaged about 40 percent.

Cisco was worried that it would unintentionally destroy the very things that made Linksys unique. For example, if Linksys used Cisco's rigorous strategic planning process, the acquired company might begin to adopt decision rules honed for Cisco's existing businesses. To avoid this problem, Cisco appointed a team of "blockers" to guard the interface between Cisco and its new division. This approach helped to minimize unintentional pollution.

Similarly, at an Innosight CEO gathering in 2007, then Best Buy CEO Brad Anderson explained his golden rule for capability-based acquisitions. He was describing how Best Buy managed to turn the tiny (less than $10 million) acquisition of a local support company called Geek Squad into a

$1 billion offering: "From the beginning, we viewed Geek Squad as having acquired Best Buy, not the other way around." The golden rule meant that Geek Squad could ask for anything it wanted from Best Buy, and Best Buy could ask nothing in return.

The second approach is to bring in select outsiders. Online video provider Hulu is a rare example of a traditional media-backed start-up (key investors include Disney, News Corp, and NBC Universal) that has created a viable, growing, disruptive business. One thing Hulu's parents did right was hiring Jason Kilar, who had experience in the online world at Amazon. Outsiders can spot points of tension that insiders might otherwise miss—and outsiders can often address that tension more aggressively.

More generally, an outsider acts as a conscious ward against the sucking sound of the core. Day 13's training described how Amazon has almost effortlessly introduced a range of innovative business models over the past decade. In an interview with Innosight, Jeff Bezos succinctly summed up his view on innovation: "If you want to really continually revitalize the service you provide the customer, you can't stop at 'What are we good at?' You have to ask, 'What do our customers need and want?' And no matter how hard it is, you better get good at those things."

The final approach is to be very precise about who has decision rights around specific processes. Many global enterprises are structured as complex matrices with specific owners for regions (e.g., Southeast Asia), functions (e.g., marketing), and product lines. This approach has operational benefits, but often places stress on innovation efforts. Innovation integrates parts of the matrix, leading to slow decision making. More critically, not every leader will be deeply intimate with the unique needs and opportunities of the new venture. Without that understanding, leaders often default to core behaviors without even realizing what they are doing.

Clear decision rights can address this challenge. Map out all of the processes involved in the innovative venture, such as marketing, distribution, production, and post-sales support. Identify who has the final say on critical decisions related to each process. There should be one decision maker. Then list all the people who should feel free to provide input but who aren't the decision maker. Tell them that that is their role. Typically, this exercise is very illuminating, because many of the input givers would otherwise assume that their input was an order.

Managing interfaces is one of the trickiest challenges facing the corporate innovator. Invest time early to get it right, or you are very likely to experience the power of the sucking sound of the core.

HOW-TO TIPS

- ✓ List the processes involved in your business. Identify three processes in which there will be tension with the core business.

- ✓ Research your company's historical growth efforts that failed. Assess whether using any of the approaches in this day's training would have helped them succeed.

Day 26
Reward Behaviors, Not Outcomes

Central Question	One-Sentence Answer
How can I motivate and reward innovation?	Shift from basing rewards on innovation outcomes to rewarding the right behaviors, even if the outcome is unsuccessful.

A few years ago, we were approached by a media company that had been on a fifteen-year tear but whose growth was starting to slow. It wanted to set up a new growth engine. The effort involved forming a small team to explore new market spaces. The group reported to the CEO and had a multimillion-dollar budget.

The company appointed an up-and-coming manager to run the growth engine. Over the next eighteen months, the manager and her team explored numerous market spaces and selected ten new business opportunities to pilot. Each venture received a small amount of seed capital to test key assumptions. Most of the pilots were shut down within six months of funding, but two demonstrated solid long-term potential, even if near-term revenues remained small. Even better, the company was developing a capability to learn about new business opportunities quickly and cheaply.

Had the growth engine leader done a good job?

Before you answer that question, consider Charlie Careful and Holly Hunch, two blackjack players you observe in Las Vegas. You watch Charlie and Holly play two hands. Miraculously, they are dealt the same cards. Each decides to bet $50 per hand. Figure 8-1 shows the action each decides to take.

FIGURE 8-1

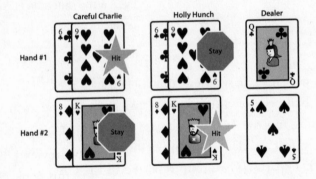

FIGURE 8-2

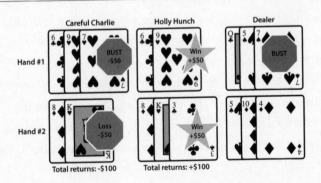

You have $1,000 in your pocket and can sponsor one of these players over the next few hours. Whom would you pick?

Before you answer, let's see how the game played out (figure 8-2). So, who gets your $1,000?

If you look at the results, you would pick Holly. She trusted her instincts, made two gutsy calls, and earned $100. However, she was incredibly lucky. The expected value of her two choices was –$58. The expected value of Charlie's was –$15.[7] Charlie appears to have followed the right decision-making process. Assuming his behavior came from an understanding of the game of blackjack, he would be a far better investment of your $1,000.

So, had the growth engine leader who had no significant commercial success done a good job? The answer is, of course, it depends.

If the assessment criterion was, "Did the manager follow *behaviors* that are consistent with innovation success?" the leader would have appropriately earned rave reviews. She followed many of the behaviors described in this book. She cost-effectively tested a range of ideas, developed a portfolio of interesting businesses, and learned a substantial amount about a range of markets.

---

7. There really is a Web site for everything. See Wizards of Odds, "Blackjack: Expected Return for Every Play," May 31, 2010, http://wizardofodds.com/blackjack/appendix1.html. A $50 bet would be expected to be worth the following, depending on whether the player stays or hits: with 15 points in the first hand and the dealer having 10, the average player could expect to lose $27.02 if he or she stayed; $25.20 if he or she hit. For the second hand, with a total of 18 points and the dealer showing 5, players could expect to win $9.98 if they stayed or to lose $30.77 if they hit.

Company management clearly took a different perspective—one Friday in 2009, it shut down the group and fired the manager. The reason? The assessment criterion that management used was, "Did the growth engine leader deliver *tangible results?*"

Most corporate readers are probably unsurprised by this outcome. Almost everyone knows that the best way to get promoted or to earn that big bonus is to hit your numbers. This approach certainly makes sense in some circumstances. A leader in a well-understood, mature business in a stable market can be safely castigated when results disappoint. It is safe to judge a worker performing a routine task according to measurable results.

But the inherently risky nature of innovation means that companies can't reward innovation efforts the way they reward core activities: an innovation team can do the exact *right* things and still fail, or succeed in spite of doing the exact *wrong* things. Worse, remember that when it comes to innovation, perceived failure is often an important step toward ultimate success. A seminal study in the mid-1980s found that that many new product "failures" were critical milestones that often presaged future successes. Typically, valuable insights came in the form of direct feedback about the viability of technology, consumer acceptance of features and pricing, and how to target new consumer segments and geographic markets.

Look again at the face of Thomas Edison on the Mount Rushmore of Innovation. Remember that it took him a thousand experiments to find an acceptable filament for the incandescent lamp. The thousand failures didn't deter Edison.

"I've gained lots of knowledge," he said. "I now know a thousand things that won't work." Naturally, punishing well-considered risks leads up-and-coming managers to play it as safe as possible to maximize their chances of long-term success.

This isn't just a corporate problem. Consider what quickly became known as Belichick's blunder. The title refers to a decision that New England Patriots football coach Bill Belichick made in a Sunday night game in November 2009. The Patriots were beating the Indianapolis Colts by six points. There were two minutes on the clock. It was fourth down. The Patriots had the ball on their own 28-yard line, two yards short of a first down that would have undoubtedly sealed the victory.

Conventional wisdom suggested a punt, but Belichick decided to go for it. The Patriots failed to convert the first down, and Indianapolis got the ball, marched into the end zone, and celebrated a stunning victory.

While pundits jumped all over Belichick, statistical research shows that Belichick actually *increased* the chances that the Patriots would win the game.

Belichick had a strong enough reputation to withstand the firestorm, but other coaches surely would hesitate before taking such a "risk" in the future. One study showed that the average professional football coach makes decisions that cost his team one win a year.[8] That's a phenomenally high number in a sixteen-game schedule!

---

8. I learned about this in Michael Mauboussin's *Think Twice*. See Pigskin Revolution, "Frequently Asked Questions," www.pigskinrevolution.com/aboutus.html.

Companies seeking to become world-class innovators have to change an often-unstated orthodoxy that pervades many corporations. They have to stop only rewarding results and start rewarding behaviors and mind-sets.

A metaphor from the quality movement helps to further illustrate this point. Companies used to spend a substantial amount of time and money conducting quality control at the *end* of a production process. The process was inherently unpredictable, they believed, so the best they could do was catch errors after they occurred and fix them. This was expensive and time-consuming. The quality movement showed that the right place to focus attention wasn't at the end of the process but at the *beginning*. If that process was set up in the right way, you could predict its results quite accurately.

Similarly, instead of looking at the end of the innovation process (results), look at the inputs into that process (behaviors). Look to see whether your managers are following behaviors that are consistent with successful intrapreneurs who skillfully blend principles of entrepreneurship with access to all the great resources inside large companies.

Also, look for ways to celebrate learning that comes from unsuccessful efforts. For example, Bessemer Venture Partners' Web site details its "anti-portfolio": all the great deals Bessemer missed. One opportunity was a "pre-IPO secondary stock at a $60M valuation" that a Bessemer leader called "outrageously expensive."[9] Thirty years later, the company—Apple—was

---

9. Bessemer Venture Partners, Portfolio, "Anti-Portfolio," www.bvp.com/Portfolio/AntiPortfolio.aspx.

worth more than $300 billion. Bessemer Venture Partners is refreshingly candid and self-effacing on its Web site: "Bessemer Venture Partners is perhaps the nation's oldest venture capital firm, carrying on an unbroken practice of venture capital investing that stretches back to 1911. This long and storied history has afforded our firm an unparalleled number of opportunities to completely screw up." Similarly, the Mayo Clinic—perhaps the world's most highly regarded medical institution—gives a "queasy eagle" award to employees who take well-thought-out risks but fail.

Even though innovation is better understood than it was a generation ago, substantial risks remain. Individuals need to recognize that failing is a critical part of their growth process, and companies need to be comfortable taking well-thought-out risks.

HOW-TO TIPS

✓ Trace the "lineage" of three successful innovation efforts inside your company. Identify past failures that were springboards to success.

✓ Send out an e-mail within the next thirty days, highlighting someone who took a risk that didn't pay off.

Day 27
Get Quick Wins

Central Question	One-Sentence Answer
How can I build momentum?	Get quick wins to ensure that efforts don't get killed when the ticking clock strikes midnight.

In early 2010, some Innosight colleagues and I were meeting with Colin Watts, the chief innovation officer of Walgreens, a $65 billion chain of U.S. drugstores. His team's mandate was to find new avenues for growth beyond Walgreens' basic strategy of spreading its stores across the United States. During the meeting, we listened as Watts described some of his efforts, and it just sounded so familiar that I had to stop and tell him, "Let me tell you about how your group could get shut down."

I told him about a financial services company Innosight had served a couple years earlier. We were working with the company's nascent innovation team. The company had formed the team about eighteen months before our engagement, and in that short period, the team had achieved a lot. It had facilitated a number of innovation workshops and helped to cultivate a portfolio of interesting growth ideas.

We helped the team further bolster that portfolio and formulate plans to implement structural changes that would help allow innovation to spread throughout the company. The ideas continued to show potential, with a reasonable estimate suggesting that they could provide more than $2 billion in revenue in just a few years.

Then, one Monday in January 2008, I received an e-mail from our main client contact: "We were fired this pm. The rest of the team will be fired tomorrow. Our boss is 'taking this in a different strategic direction.'"

At first glance, this seems ridiculous. Developing a massive portfolio in two years is an incredible accomplishment.

The team's problem was quite simple. While the team members had helped nurture ideas with a tremendous amount of *potential*, they hadn't affected near-term *performance*. And when the financial services company (correctly) saw that its base business faced impending difficulty, it was easy to chop the innovation team.[10]

In financial terms, the company's leadership team decided that the rate at which it discounted future, uncertain dollars was infinite. In simple terms, the leadership would prefer to have a certain amount of dollars today over any amount of dollars in the future.

Innovation master Clayton Christensen describes this concept as the "ticking clock." You never know quite how fast the clock is ticking, or when the alarm is set, but you can be darn sure that at some point, it will ring. The proverbial

---

10. No, I am not naming names here, either. I will just say that this was *not* a company that went on to receive bailouts. It actually did quite well in 2008 and 2009.

clock always strikes midnight. If that moment comes and all you have is potential, you'd better start polishing your résumé.

Watts is a smart guy, so he instantly understood the implications of my story. "I better get some quick wins, huh?" he said. As we talked about it further, we thought it made strategic sense to redirect some resources focused on an exciting but uncertain project into something that would generate immediate results that would benefit the core business. Specifically, Watts picked up an effort that had been on the corporate to-do list for a decade. Implementing this project would, when the ticking clock struck midnight, protect Watts by generating powerful proof that this "innovation thing" could have positive impact in the company.

If you are an innovation leader inside a company, think about how you can accelerate the path to get "points on the board." Is there a project that one of the established parts of the organization is struggling to get done? Is there an agreed-upon strategic imperative that has languished for years? Could you push one of the ideas you are working on to get to market sooner, even if it means making it smaller? Is there a small deal you can strike with another company to do something as simple as cobranding a product or service? If you are working on an individual effort, can you do something in thirty days that builds your own confidence?

It's unlikely that these kinds of efforts are the sorts that will land you or your organization on the front page of the *Wall Street Journal* or TechCrunch.com. They will, however, provide "air cover" to support more expansive efforts and build confidence in the long-term value of further investment.

HOW-TO TIPS

- ✓ Identify an effort that could produce results that leaders in the core business would consider positive in the next six months.

- ✓ Identify a thirty-day milestone that would demonstrate the value of further investment.

- ✓ Survey a handful of core business leaders to find out what's keeping them up at night to identify potential "quick win" opportunities.

Day 28
Practice Makes Perfect

Central Question	One-Sentence Answer
How can I become systematically better at innovation?	Put yourself in circumstances where you *have* to practice core innovation skills.

Innovation is a discipline. Individuals can get better at it. Corporations can systematize it. The final day's training describes how to strengthen your innovation muscles.

The innovation sin of lust detailed in chapter 4 detailed how Willy Shih cautioned us about the "bright, shiny object problem." Shih taught us another important lesson that day. He asked us to list the important initiatives that Innosight was undertaking. He then asked us to create a separate list of the important initiatives that Innosight was undertaking and that we individually were working on.[11] Some of the so-called important initiatives were on *none* of our lists.

---

11. Ms. Sussman, my eighth-grade English teacher, would be sad that I ended a sentence with a preposition. But I would tell Ms. Sussman that Winston Churchill, upon seeing one of his sentences changed so as not to end with a preposition, allegedly wrote, "This is the sort of bloody nonsense up with which I will not put." There seems to be a Churchill story for every occasion (whether this story is true or not is unclear); see Paul Brians, "Ending a Sentence with a Preposition," in *Common Errors in English Usage*, http://public.wsu.edu/~brians/errors/errors.txt.

"Where you spend your time is a reflection of your priorities," Shih told us.

Remember, innovation is a skill. And like all skills, the more you practice, the sharper the skill. If innovation is important to you, your department, your group, or your company, you have to dedicate the time to get better at it.

The best innovators train. Much of this training is subconscious. We all have read stories of the "serial entrepreneurs" who bounce from one opportunity to another. Along the way, they are learning what works and what doesn't work. I tell consulting teams that every project we do should be our absolute best project, because we can draw on accumulated knowledge that the teams before us could not access.

Training can be conscious as well. Specifically, look to put yourself in circumstances that force you to exercise core innovation skills.

Consider the example of Fred Brushley.[12] I first met Brushley in 2005, when he was an up-and-coming middle manager inside a pretty large global company. He had two distinct jobs within that company. One job involved managing one of the company's core product lines. The other job involved heading up new business building activities inside one of the company's large business units. He and his small team had responsibility for identifying and developing new ideas that would otherwise fall between the organizational cracks.

---

12. Fred Brushley is a pseudonym, and the story is disguised a bit to protect the protagonist, who was a bit worried that his company might not be so keen on his experiment.

On a daily basis, Brushley was telling the teams he oversaw to be more entrepreneurial, to be more innovative. He thought to himself, "I can't give this kind of advice if I haven't *lived* like an entrepreneur." So he and his brother formed a small side business—an online venture that provided packaged deals for experiential tours of California's wine region. Brushley made sure that the outside venture didn't affect his "day job," and the experience gave him direct exposure to the common challenges of growth and innovation, increasing his ability to give cogent advice to his teams.

You don't have to start a new business to brush up against entrepreneurialism. Close to 10 million people in the United States alone are self-employed. Find a friend or family member who is going at it alone, and see if you can't engage with this person to learn about the challenges he or she is facing. For example, I have learned a tremendous amount from watching, and too infrequently participating in, my sister's efforts to start her own businesses.

Of course, one of the best ways to train is to try to teach someone a concept. Pay careful attention to questions from "students." Great questions will help you connect concepts in different ways and put your antenna up for pertinent case examples or research. I estimate that about 50 percent of my blog posts come from questions posed by audience members at speeches or workshops.

Read as much as time will allow. Look for stories describing new product launches or strategic shifts where some of the approaches described in this book might provide insight.

Jot down a few thoughts about what the models let you see. It's just another way to work that innovation muscle. Similarly, consider forming a lunchtime (or virtual) discussion group where you and your colleagues discuss relevant innovation topics. Spend time discussing the latest hot start-up. Do a Lincoln-Douglas style of debate, in which you develop arguments for why a company will succeed and why it will fail.

People who are hungry for even more suggestions should turn to the research of Jeffrey Dyer and Hal Gregersen. The two professors have spent years decoding the innovator's DNA. Their research and writing provide dozens of practical suggestions for how people can become better innovators. One of my favorite pieces of advice is to find ways to "consciously complicate" your life. For example, pick up a magazine in a field with which you are unfamiliar. Or attend a trade show that seems to have nothing to do with your job. Keep forcing yourself to seek the intersections between the new experience and your current challenge. The professors also cite research that shows how people who spend a substantial amount of time living in a foreign country are notably better innovators. Any form of ex-pat assignment has its challenges, but it also exposes you to stimuli that you could not otherwise experience.

Some of the guidance here might sound daunting because it involves reshaping routines and seeking out new experiences. But no one became great at anything without substantial work.

HOW-TO TIPS

✓ Make a list of everyone you know who is self-employed or working at a company with fewer than ten people. Send an e-mail to see if any of them could use free advice.

✓ Clip two stories out of a newspaper or magazine where the concepts described in this book let you see something that was otherwise hidden.

✓ Create a thirty-day innovation training program.

Week 4 Wrap-Up

The focus of week 4 was moving forward in your innovation journey. You should have answered four questions:

1. How can I use selective scarcity and external resources to accelerate innovation?

2. What should I borrow, and what should I forget?

3. How can I block the sucking sound of the core?

4. What can I do to improve my innovation capabilities?

More broadly, remember three critical phrases:

1. Selective scarcity: Intentionally imposing constraints can enable innovation.

2. Sucking sound of the core: Left unchecked, a company's core business or your core skills can unintentionally limit an idea's potential.

3. Behavior, not results: The uncertain nature of innovation means that rewards should focus more on the behaviors innovators follow than the results they obtain.

THE INNOVATOR'S PLEDGE

If you have followed the 28-day innovation program, or embraced the philosophies that lie behind them, you have begun to stretch the bonds of the status quo. You are on your way to fully breaking them and becoming a full-fledged innovator. Table C-1 serves as a simple reminder of the key lessons from each stage of the program.

To reinforce those lessons, consider taking the Innovator's Pledge, which borrows from the Declaration of Independence and the pledge that I and other safety patrols had to recite every day at Luxmanor Elementary School (where my political career ended after my crushing loss in the third-grade vice president election).[1]

The pledge begins with a statement:

> We hold these truths to be self-evident, that all
> have the ability to innovate, that they are endowed

---

1. "I promise to do my best to . . . report for duty on time, perform my duties faithfully, strive to prevent accidents, always setting a good example myself, obey my teachers and officers of the patrol, report dangerous student practices, strive to earn the respect of fellow students." Thanks, World Wide Web!

with certain unalienable Capabilities, that among
these are Curiosity, Creativity, and the pursuit of
Growth.

I really do believe this statement. Everyone has the ability
to be a successful innovator.

Next come seven simple ways to reinforce the lessons that
have run through this book:

I promise to do my best to:

- Triple the time I spend with the customers.

- Routinely ask "Why?" "Why not?" and "What if?"

- Strive to run an experiment a day.

- Always look for ways to learn more without spending
  money.

- Get to the intersections.

- Call up the most iconoclastic person I know and ask to
  be introduced to the most iconoclastic person he or she
  knows.

- Teach a friend three key innovation lessons.

Following the Innovator's Pledge will reinforce what you
practiced during my twenty-eight-day program. Best of luck
to you in your innovation efforts!

TABLE C-1

The Little Black Book's 28 Day Innovation Program

	Day	Daily tip	Central question	One-sentence answer
Week 1: Discovering	1	Start Before You Need To	How do I know it is time to innovate?	Watch for early warning signs, because the urgency of innovation and the ability to innovate are inversely related.
	2	Remember, the Consumer Is Boss	How do I spot opportunities for innovation?	Take a consumer-is-boss perspective.
	3	Get the Job Done	What indicates an opportunity for innovation?	Look for an important, unsatisfied job to be done, or a problem the customer can't adequately address today.
	4	Compete Against Nonconsumption	Which customers should I target?	Look for "nonconsumers" that face a barrier inhibiting their ability to get a job done.
	5	Find Compensating Behaviors	How can I find nonobvious opportunities?	Consider targeting the compensating behavior that an individual follows to cover the inadequacy of existing solutions.
	6	Get as Close to Context as Possible	How should I investigate potential opportunities?	Start with deep observational or ethnographic research; avoid focus groups like the plague.
	7	Don't Innovate Blind	How can I confirm that the opportunity I have spotted is real?	Invest the time to understand the market you hope to target—always ask why smart people haven't seized an opportunity that looks obvious to you.

TABLE C-1 (Continued)

The Little Black Book's 28 Day Innovation Program

Day	Daily tip	Central question	One-sentence answer
8	Go to the Intersections	How can I get inspiration for an idea?	Go to the intersections, and borrow liberally from other contexts.
9	Seek Ideas from Everywhere	Where should I look for inspiration?	Rapidly explore as many avenues as possible when searching for new ideas.
10	Remember: Quality Is Relative	Is my idea high quality?	Quality is a relative term that can only be determined by understanding what matters to the target customer.
11	Avoid Overshooting	Is there such a thing as too good?	It is possible to overshoot your target market by introducing features that the customer will take, but not value enough to pay for.
12	Do It Differently	What is a disruptive innovation?	Disruptive innovations create new markets and transform existing ones through simplicity, convenience, affordability, or accessibility.
13	Embrace Business Model Innovation	What is a business model, and how do I innovate it?	A business model describes how a company creates, captures, and delivers value; systematically considering a wide range of business model options can help enable business model innovation.
14	Bring It Together	How can I translate my work into a concrete blueprint?	"Don't just do something—stand there"; step back and summarize your work in a comprehensive plan.

Week 2: Blueprinting Ideas

Week 3: Assessing and Testing Ideas

15	Let Patterns Guide and Actions Decide	How can I separate good ideas from bad ideas?	Use patterns to get a directional sense as to whether an idea is any good, and then run experiments to confirm that directional sense.
16	Calculate Your Idea's Four *P*'s	What is a quick way to estimate my idea's financial potential?	Multiply population, penetration, price, and purchase frequency to gain quick insight into an idea's potential.
17	Reverse-Engineer Success	How can I identify an idea's most critical assumptions?	Determine what success looks like, and then identify the two most critical things that would have to happen for success to be obtainable.
18	Test Critical Assumptions	How can I learn more about my idea?	Tests are the best ways to learn about existing critical assumptions and to identify new ones.
19	Bring Ideas to Life	How can I get people behind my idea?	Find creative ways to bring ideas to life in order to build buy-in and motivate action.
20	Embrace Everyday Experimentation	How can I get good at experimenting?	Be on constant lookout for ways to run everyday experiments.
21	Savor Surprises	How can I learn the right things from my experiments?	Experience the raw data, and focus on the findings you did not expect.

TABLE C-1 (Continued)

The Little Black Book's 28 Day Innovation Program

Day	Daily tip	Central question	One-sentence answer
22	Embrace Selective Scarcity	How much should I invest in innovation?	Embrace selective scarcity with tight timelines, single decision makers, and constrained strategic choices.
23	Amplify Your Resources	Where can I find resources for innovation?	Leverage external resources, and redirect currently committed resources.
24	Break the Sucking Sound of the Core	How can I avoid the sucking sound of the core?	Active leadership, new voices, safe spaces, and smart borrowing can help protect innovators from the sucking sound of the core.
25	Manage the Interfaces	How do I manage interfaces between a new business and the core business?	Use a range of techniques to make sure you don't accidentally remember what you are trying to forget.
26	Reward Behaviors, Not Outcomes	How can I motivate and reward innovation?	Shift from basing rewards on innovation outcomes to rewarding the right behaviors, even if the outcome is unsuccessful.
27	Get Quick Wins	How can I build momentum?	Get quick wins to ensure that efforts don't get killed when the ticking clock strikes midnight.
28	Practice Makes Perfect	How can I become systematically better at innovation?	Put yourself in circumstances where you *have* to practice core innovation skills.

Week 4: Moving Forward

APPENDIX

BEYOND THE INNOVATION MASTERS

Clearly, the twelve innovation masters mentioned in chapter 2 don't have a monopoly on interesting ideas. Some books you are likely to find most helpful include the following:

- Dan Ariely, *Predictably Irrational: The Hidden Forces That Shape Our Decisions* (New York: Harper, 2008) (a very accessible entry point into behavioral psychology)

- Amar Bhidé, *The Origin and Evolution of New Businesses* (New York: Oxford University Press, 2000) (lots of information about the reality of starting businesses up)

- Robert Burgelman, *Strategy Is Destiny: How Strategy-Making Shapes a Company's Future* (New York: Free Press, 2002) (explains the principle of emergent strategy in great detail)

- Chip Heath and Dan Heath, *Made to Stick: Why Some Ideas Survive and Others Die* (New York: Random

House, 2007) (how to communicate concepts in ways that make them stick); and Chip Heath and Dan Heath, *Switch: How to Change Things When Change Is Hard* (New York: Broadway Books, 2010) (how to drive behavior change)

- Guy Kawasaki, *The Art of the Start: The Time-Tested, Battle-Hardened Guide for Anyone Starting Anything* (New York: Portfolio, 2004) (tips and tricks for starting a new business); Guy Kawasaki, "How to Change the World: A Practical Blog for Impractical People," http://blog.guykawasaki.com/ (Kawasaki's popular blog); and anything else written by Kawasaki

- W. Chan Kim and Renée Mauborgne, *Blue Ocean Strategy: How to Create Uncontested Market Space and Make the Competition Irrelevant* (Boston: Harvard Business School Press, 2005) (additional thoughts and tools to help innovators spot new market spaces)

- Mark W. Johnson, *Seizing the White Space: Business Model Innovation for Growth and Renewal* (Boston: Harvard Business Press, 2010) (Johnson is a colleague and a friend, but his book is a legitimately great read on the important topic of business model innovation)

- David Kord Murray, *Borrowing Brilliance: The Six Steps to Business Innovation by Building on the Ideas of Others* (New York: Gotham Books, 2009) (as good a book as I've seen on using simple principles to come up with ideas)

- Alexander Osterwalder and Yves Pigneur, *Business Model Generation: A Handbook for Visionaries, Game Changers, and Challengers* (New Jersey: John Wiley & Sons, 2010) (wonderfully designed book with a good set of tools to foster the creation of new business models)

- Philip Rosenzweig, *The Halo Effect . . . and the Eight Other Business Delusions That Deceive Managers* (New York: Free Press, 2007) (thoughtful critique that debunks the findings in a range of seemingly scholarly business books)

- Peter Sims, *Little Bets: How Breakthrough Ideas Emerge from Small Discoveries* (New York: Free Press, 2011) (highly accessible book describing the principles of "emergent strategy")

People interested in learning more about the topics covered in the twenty-eight-day innovation program should check out the following books (note some of these overlap with books mentioned elsewhere in *The Little Black Book*).

WEEK 1: DISCOVERING OPPORTUNITIES

- Steven Johnson, *Where Good Ideas Come From: The Natural History of Innovation* (New York: Riverhead Books, 2010)

- A. G. Lafley and Ram Charan, *The Game-Changer: How You Can Drive Revenue and Profit Growth with Innovation* (New York: Crown Business, 2008)

- Charlene Li and Josh Bernoff, *Groundswell: Winning in a World Transformed by Social Technologies* (Boston: Harvard Business School Press, 2008)

- Clotaire Rapaille, *The Culture Code: An Ingenious Way to Understand Why People Around the World Buy and Live as They Do* (New York: Broadway Books, 2007)

- Gerald Zaltman, *How Customers Think: Essential Insights into the Mind of the Market* (Boston: Harvard Business School Press, 2003)

WEEK 2: BLUEPRINT IDEAS

- Scott D. Anthony et al., *The Innovator's Guide to Growth: Putting Disruptive Innovation to Work* (Boston: Harvard Business Press, 2008), especially chapter 5, "Developing Disruptive Ideas"

- Chip Heath and Dan Heath, *Made to Stick: Why Some Ideas Survive and Others Die* (New York: Random House, 2007)

- Frans Johansson, *The Medici Effect: Breakthrough Insights at the Intersection of Ideas, Concepts, and Cultures* (Boston: Harvard Business School Press, 2004)

- Steven Johnson, *Where Good Ideas Come From: The Natural History of Innovation* (New York: Riverhead Books, 2010)

- W. Chan Kim and Renée Mauborgne, *Blue Ocean Strategy: How to Create Uncontested Market Space and Make the Competition Irrelevant* (Boston: Harvard Business School Press, 2005)

- David Kord Murray, *Borrowing Brilliance: The Six Steps to Business Innovation by Building on the Ideas of Others* (New York: Gotham Books, 2009)

- Alexander Osterwalder and Yves Pigneur, *Business Model Generation: A Handbook for Visionaries, Game Changers, and Challengers* (New Jersey: John Wiley & Sons, 2010)

WEEK 3: ASSESSING AND TESTING IDEAS

- Steven Gary Blank, *Four Steps to the Epiphany* (San Mateo, CA: Cafepress.com, 2005)

- Vijay Govindarajan and Chris Trimble, *The Other Side of Innovation: Solving the Execution Challenge* (Boston: Harvard Business Press, 2010)

- Rita Gunther McGrath and Ian C. MacMillan, *Discovery-Driven Growth: A Breakthrough Process to Reduce Risk and Seize Opportunity* (Boston: Harvard Business Press, 2009)

- John Mullins and Randy Komisar, *Getting to Plan B: Breaking Through to a Better Business Model* (Boston: Harvard Business Press, 2009)

Appendix

WEEK 4: MOVING FORWARD

- Scott D. Anthony et al., *The Innovator's Guide to Growth: Putting Disruptive Innovation to Work* (Boston: Harvard Business School Press, 2008)

- Clayton M. Christensen and Michael E. Raynor, *The Innovator's Solution: Creating and Sustaining Successful Growth* (Boston: Harvard Business School Press, 2003)

- Jeffrey Dyer, Hal Gregersen, and Clayton Christensen, *The Innovator's DNA: Mastering the Five Skills of Disruptive Innovators* (Boston: Harvard Business Review Press, 2011)

- Richard N. Foster and Sarah Kaplan, *Creative Destruction: Why Companies That Are Built to Last Underperform the Market, and How to Successfully Transform Them* (New York: Currency/Doubleday, 2001)

- Vijay Govindarajan and Chris Trimble, *Ten Rules for Strategic Innovators: From Idea to Execution* (Boston: Harvard Business School Press, 2005)

- Guy Kawasaki, *The Art of the Start: The Time-Tested, Battle-Hardened Guide for Anyone Starting Anything* (New York: Portfolio, 2004)

- Morgan McCall, *High Flyers: Developing the Next Generation of Leaders* (Boston: Harvard Business School Press, 1998)

Appendix

- Michael L. Tushman and Charles A. O'Reilly III, *Winning Through Innovation: A Practical Guide to Leading Organizational Change and Renewal* (Boston: Harvard Business School Press, 2002)

NOTES

Introduction: My Innovation Journey

The Dartmouth's Internet strategy: Charles Davant, "The D, Launching On-Line Version, Enters Cyberspace," *The Dartmouth*, May 23, 1995, http://thedartmouth.com/1995/05/23/news/the.

Chapter 1: The Innovation Imperative

Background on Thomas Edison: Randall E. Stross, *The Wizard of Menlo Park: How Thomas Alva Edison Invented the Modern World* (New York: Crown, 2007).

Definitions of innovation: Hutch Carpenter, "25 Definitions of Innovation," *Blogging Innovation*, August 25, 2010, www.business-strategy-innovation.com/wordpress/2010/08/25-definitions-of-innovation/.

Accounting Hall of Fame: Fisher College of Business, Ohio State University, "The Accounting Hall of Fame," http://fisher.osu.edu/departments/accounting-and-mis/the-accounting-hall-of-fame/.

Procter & Gamble definitions of innovation: Bruce Brown and Scott D. Anthony, "How P&G Tripled Its Innovation Success Rate," *Harvard Business Review*, June 2010.

"Strategic inflection points offer promises as well as threats": Andrew S. Grove, *Only the Paranoid Survive: How to Exploit the Crisis Points That Challenge Every Company* (New York: Currency, 1996).

Shortening corporate life span: Richard N. Foster and Sarah Kaplan, *Creative Destruction: Why Companies That Are Built to Last Underperform the Market—And How to Successfully Transform Them* (New York: Currency/Doubleday, 2001).

Holly's laptop: Scott D. Anthony, "Lessons from My Daughter's Laptop," *Harvard Business Review Blog Network*, April 14, 2011, http://blogs.hbr.org/anthony/2011/04/lessons_from_my_daughters_lapt.html.

Notes

Parenting case study: William A. Sahlman, "Parenting Magazine," Case 9-291-015 (Boston: Harvard Business School, 1990).

Innovator's DNA work: Jeffrey Dyer, Hal Gregersen, and Clayton M. Christensen, "The Innovator's DNA," *Harvard Business Review*, December 2009; and Jeffrey Dyer, Hal Gregersen, and Clayton M. Christensen, *The Innovator's DNA: Mastering the Five Skills of Disruptive Innovators* (Boston: Harvard Business Review Press, 2011).

Hollywood pitch: Chip Heath and Dan Heath, *Made to Stick: Why Some Ideas Survive and Others Die* (New York: Random House, 2007).

Chapter 2: The Masters of Innovation

Steve Blank: Steve Gary Blank, *Four Steps to the Epiphany* (San Mateo, CA: Cafepress.com, 2005).

Clayton Christensen: Clayton M. Christensen, *The Innovator's Dilemma: When New Technologies Cause Great Firms to Fail* (Boston: Harvard Business School Press, 1997); Clayton M. Christensen and Michael E. Raynor, *The Innovator's Solution: Creating and Sustaining Successful Growth* (Boston: Harvard Business School Press, 2003); Clayton M. Christensen, Scott D. Anthony, and Erik A. Roth, *Seeing What's Next: Using Theories of Innovation to Predict Industry Change* (Boston: Harvard Business School Press, 2004); Clayton M. Christensen, Curtis W. Johnson, and Michael B. Horn, *Disrupting Class: How Disruptive Innovation Will Change the Way the World Learns* (New York: McGraw-Hill, 2008); Clayton M. Christensen, Jason Hwang, and Jerome Grossman, *The Innovator's Prescription: A Disruptive Solution for Health Care* (New York: McGraw-Hill, 2009).

Peter Drucker: Peter F. Drucker, "The Discipline of Innovation," *Harvard Business Review*, May–June 1985; Peter F. Drucker, *Innovation and Entrepreneurship* (New York: HarperCollins, 1985).

Thomas Alva Edison: Stross, *The Wizard of Menlo Park*.

Richard Foster: Foster and Kaplan, *Creative Destruction*; Richard N. Foster, *Innovation: The Attacker's Advantage* (New York: Summit Books, 1986).

Notes

Vijay Govindarajan: Vijay Govindarajan and Chris Trimble, *Ten Rules for Strategic Innovators: From Idea to Execution* (Boston: Harvard Business School Press, 2005); Vijay Govindarajan and Chris Trimble, *The Other Side of Innovation: Solving the Execution Challenge* (Boston: Harvard Business School Press, 2010); Jeffrey R. Immelt, Vijay Govindarajan, and Chris Trimble, "How GE Is Disrupting Itself," *Harvard Business Review*, October 2009.

Bill James: Bill James, *The New Bill James Historical Baseball Abstract* (New York: Free Press, 2001); Scott D. Anthony, "Major League Innovation," *Harvard Business Review*, October 2009.

A. G. Lafley: A. G. Lafley and Ram Charan, *The Game-Changer: How You Can Drive Revenue and Profit Growth with Innovation* (New York: Random House, 2008); A. G. Lafley, "What Only the CEO Can Do," *Harvard Business Review*, May 2009.

Roger Martin: Roger L. Martin, *The Opposable Mind: How Successful Leaders Win Through Integrative Thinking* (Boston: Harvard Business Press, 2007); Roger L. Martin, *The Design of Business: Why Design Thinking Is the Next Competitive Advantage* (Boston: Harvard Business Press, 2009).

Michael Mauboussin: Michael J. Mauboussin, *More Than You Know: Finding Financial Wisdom in Conventional Places* (New York: Columbia University Press, 2007); Michael J. Mauboussin, *Think Twice: Harnessing the Power of Counterintuition* (Boston: Harvard Business Press, 2009).

Rita McGrath: Rita Gunther McGrath and Ian C. MacMillan, "Discovery-Driven Planning," *Harvard Business Review*, July–August 1995; Rita Gunther McGrath and Ian C. MacMillan, *Discovery-Driven Growth: A Breakthrough Process to Reduce Risk and Seize Opportunity* (Boston: Harvard Business Press, 2009).

Joseph Schumpeter: Joseph R. Schumpeter, *Capitalism, Socialism, and Democracy* (New York: Harper & Brothers, 1942).

Chapter 3: The Mount Rushmore of Innovation

"The customer rarely buys": Peter F. Drucker, *Managing for Results* (London: William Heinemann Ltd., 1964).

Notes

Various Edison quotes: Gerald Beals, "Thomas Alva Edison 'Quotes,'" Thomas Alva Edison, American Inventor, 1847–1931, Web site, 1996, www.thomasedison.com/quotes.html.

"What Facebook did was people-centric, not photo-centric": James Joaquin, quoted in Jefferson Graham, "Facebook's 'Tagging' Option Is a Big Hit with Photo Sharing," *USA Today*, September 23, 2009, www.usatoday.com/tech/news/2009-09-22-facebook-photo-sharing-tagging_N.htm.

Chapter 4: Innovation's Seven Deadly Sins

The Economist chart about the number of blades: "The Cutting Edge," *The Economist*, March 16, 2006, www.economist.com/node/5624861?story_id=5624861.

Sin of gluttony: James Clayton, Bradley Gambill, and Douglas Harned, "The Curse of Too Much Capital: Building New Businesses in Large Corporations," *McKinsey Quarterly*, no. 3 (August 1999).

Sin of envy: Govindarajan and Trimble, *The Other Side of Innovation*.

Sin of wrath: Daniel Pink, *Drive: The Surprising Truth About What Motivates Us* (New York: Riverhead Books, 2009).

Week 1: Discovering Opportunities

Day 1

Information about the post office: Scott D. Anthony, "The Key to Spotting Disruption Before It Happens," *Harvard Business Review Blog Network*, May 4, 2010, http://blogs.hbr.org/anthony/2010/05/the_key_to_spotting_disruption.html.

Growth-gap death spiral: Christensen and Raynor, *The Innovator's Solution*, chapter 9.

"By the time the writing is on the wall": Christensen et al., *Seeing What's Next*, conclusion.

Faraci at newspaper industry conference: Rich Edmonds, "Timely Tough Love for the Industry," PoynterOnline, April 15, 2008, http://legacy2.poynter.org/column.asp?id=123&aid=141581.

Notes

Day 2

Lafley quote: The quote was from a discussion with the author at the May 2008 PDMA and IIR Front End of Innovation conference in Boston. A summary version of this conversation appears in Scott D. Anthony, "Game-Changing at Procter & Gamble," *Strategy + Innovation* 6, no. 4 (2008), www.innosight.com/documents/protected/SI/JulyAugust2008StrategyandInnovation.pdf. For a full transcript, e-mail the author at santhony@innosight.com.

Day 3

Job-to-be done lens: Clayton M. Christensen, Scott D. Anthony, Gerald Berstell, and Denise Nitterhouse, "Finding the Right Job for Your Product," *MIT Sloan Management Review* 48, no. 3 (2007).

"The customer rarely buys": Drucker, *Managing for Results*.

Day 4

Different types of nonconsumption: W. Chan Kim and Renée Mauborgne, *Blue Ocean Strategy: How to Create Uncontested Market Space and Make the Competition Irrelevant* (Boston: Harvard Business School Press, 2005); Christensen and Raynor, *The Innovator's Solution*, chapter 4; C. K. Prahalad, *The Fortune at the Bottom of the Pyramid: Eradicating Poverty Through Profits* (Upper Saddle River, NJ: Wharton School Publishing, 2006).

ChotuKool story: Matthew J. Eyring, Mark W. Johnson, and Hari Nair, "New Business Models in Emerging Markets," *Harvard Business Review*, January–February 2011.

Day 5

Tata Nano story: Mark W. Johnson, *Seizing the White Space: Business Model Innovation for Growth and Renewal* (Boston: Harvard Business Press, 2010); Scott D. Anthony, "Is the Tata Nano Really 'The People's Car'?" *Harvard Business Review Blog Network*, November 13, 2009, http://blogs.hbr.org/anthony/2009/11/is_the_nano_really_the_peoples.html.

Day 6

"Do the job of discovering the job": Scott D. Anthony et al., *The Innovator's Guide to Growth: Putting Disruptive Innovation to Work* (Boston: Harvard Business School Press, 2008), chapter 4.

Notes

Week 2: Blueprinting Ideas

Day 8

Adapting and adopting from another field: David Kord Murray, *Borrowing Brilliance: The Six Steps to Business Innovation by Building on the Ideas of Others* (New York: Penguin Group, 2009).

Background on MinuteClinic: Richard Bohmer and Jonathan P. Groberg, "QuickMedx, Inc.," Case 9-603-049 (Boston: Harvard Business School, 2002).

Day 9

Netflix contest: Steve Lohr, "A $1 Million Research Bargain for Netflix, and Maybe a Model for Others," *New York Times*, September 21, 2009, www.nytimes.com/2009/09/22/technology/internet/22netflix.html.

Day 10

Strategy canvas: Kim and Mauborgne, *Blue Ocean Strategy*; see also Anthony et al., *The Innovator's Guide to Growth*, 130.

Day 11

Telephone service example: Anthony et al., *The Innovator's Guide to Growth*, 69.

Gillette example: Ellen Byron, "Gillette Sharpens Its Pitch for Expensive Razor," *Wall Street Journal*, October 6, 2008, http://online.wsj.com/article/SB122325275682206367.html.

Gillette Guard example: Brown and Anthony, "How P&G Tripled Its Innovation Success Rate."

Day 12

Overview of disruptive technology: Christensen, *The Innovator's Dilemma*; Christensen and Raynor, *The Innovator's Solution*.

Day 13

Apple revenues: Figures from Apple's financial filings, available at http://investor.apple.com/sec.cfm.

Definition of business model: Johnson, *Seizing the White Space*.

Notes

Day 14

Idea résumé: Anthony et al., *The Innovator's Guide to Growth*, 129.

Week 3: Assessing and Testing Ideas

Day 15

"For every one of our failures": Scott Cook, quoted in Jena McGregor, "How Failure Breeds Success," *BusinessWeek*, July 10, 2006.

Day 16

Original four *P*'s article: Scott D. Anthony, "The 4 *P*'s of Innovation," *Harvard Business Review Blog Network*, June 10, 2010, blogs.hbr.org/anthony/2010/06/the_4ps_of_innovation.htm.

Day 17

Discovery-driven planning process: McGrath and MacMillan, *Discovery-Driven Growth*.

Day 18

Integrated experiments: Clark G. Gilbert and Matthew J. Eyring, "Beating the Odds When You Launch a New Venture," *Harvard Business Review*, May 2010.

TVinContext story: Scott D. Anthony, *The Silver Lining: An Innovation Playbook for Uncertain Times* (Boston: Harvard Business Press, 2009), 103–104.

Day 19

Hollywood pitch: Heath and Heath, *Made to Stick*.

Day 20

Dow Corning thought experiment: Johnson, *Seizing the White Space*, 59.

Coffee story: Scott D. Anthony, "Innovators: Become Active Experimenters," *Harvard Business Review Blog Network*, March 29, 2010, http://blogs.hbr.org/anthony/2010/03/innovators_become_active_experimenters.html.

Notes

Day 21

Confirmation bias example: A. H. Hastorf and H. Cantril, "They Saw a Game: A Case Study," *Journal of Abnormal and Social Psychology* 49 (1954): 129–134.

Wisdom of crowds: Don Tapscott and Anthony D. Williams, *Wikinomics: How Mass Collaboration Changes Everything* (New York: Penguin Group, 2006); James Surowiecki, *The Wisdom of Crowds* (Anchor: Garden City, NY, 2005).

Week 4: Moving Forward

Day 22

Benefits of scarcity on innovation: Anthony, *The Silver Lining.*

Downside of abundance: Clayton et al., "Curse of Too Much Capital."

Heath brothers' thought experiment: Heath and Heath, *Made to Stick*, 119–120.

Goals and bounds tool: Anthony et al., *The Innovators' Guide to Growth*, 27–30.

Day 23

Richard Foster's research: Foster and Kaplan, *Creative Destruction.*

R&R case study: Howard M. Stevenson and Jose-Carlos Jarillo Mossi, "R&R," Case 9-386-019 (Boston: Harvard Business School, 1985); Anthony, *The Silver Lining*, chapter 6.

Day 24

Core competence: C. K. Prahalad and Gary Hamel, "The Core Competence of the Corporation," *Harvard Business Review*, May–June 1990.

Xiameter study: Johnson, *Seizing the White Space*, chapter 3.

Day 25

Microsoft story: Robert A. Guth, "Microsoft Bid to Beat Google Builds on a History of Misses," *Wall Street Journal*, January 16, 2009; Scott

Notes

D. Anthony, "Microsoft: Letting Disruption Slip Through Its Fingers," *Harvard Business Review Blog Network*, January 16, 2009, http://blogs.hbr.org/anthony/2009/01/microsoft_letting_disruption_s.html.

Linksys and Brad Anderson stories: Anthony et al., *The Innovator's Guide to Growth*, chapter 8.

"If you want to really continually revitalize the service": Jeff Bezos, interview with Innosight, October 13, 2008.

Day 26

Study on failures: M. A. Maidique and B. J. Zirger, "New Product Learning Cycle," *Research Policy* 14 (1985): 299–313.

Football coaches making suboptimal decisions: Mauboussin, *Think Twice*. See also Pigskin Revolution, "Frequently Asked Questions," www.pigskinrevolution.com/aboutus.html.

Day 27

Christensen's "ticking clock": Christensen and Raynor, *The Innovator's Solution*, chapter 9.

Day 28

Innovator's DNA: Dyer, Gregersen, and Christensen, *The Innovator's DNA*.

INDEX

Index

ACKNOWLEDGMENTS

People who have read my previous books will recognize that *The Little Black Book of Innovation* has a distinct style. This style shift was an intentional attempt on my part to make the concepts I was describing more accessible. To maximize my chances of success, I enlisted the support of a handful of trusted advisors. I owe particular thanks to three of them: Michelle Anthony (one of my sisters), Lib Gibson, and Karl Ronn. Michelle provided incredibly helpful and detailed comments during two rapid-fire editing rounds in late 2010. As a self-proclaimed innovation novice, she helped make sure that the book explained things clearly, without too much jargon. Michelle also demonstrated a keen eye for where the first-person voice became unintentionally off-putting. Lib gave me candid, direct, and immensely valuable feedback about the first version of the manuscript. (I summarized that feedback to my wife simply as, "She hated it.") Lib also gave me detailed guidance about how to modulate my tone so that the book didn't come across as arrogant or dismissive. The idea for the twenty-eight day innovation program came from Lib, and she gave her blessing to the final manuscript—though she said her favorite of my small collection remains *The Silver Lining*. Karl's comments—delivered as "an early Christmas present" in mid-December—were so useful they made it directly into the manuscript in several places. His unique perspective is always valuable. The team at Harvard Business Review Publishing, notably Tim Sullivan, Kevin Evers, Stephani Finks, and Allison Peter, provided its usual great support throughout the process. Special thanks to Kathleen Carr for starting the journey with me before she transitioned to her new role at Simmons College.

My deep thanks to the truly amazing team at Innosight. I feel privileged to be associated with all of you. I hope I have effectively channeled the great work done by so many project teams and the great thinking and writing by Innosight's expanding stable of home-grown thought leaders. Special thanks go to Matthew Eyring, Mark Johnson, Joe Sinfield, Jim Dougherty, Kevin Bolen, Cathy Olofson, Tara Young, Hari Nair, and Pete Bonee for reasons each of you know well.

The companies I have had the honor of serving, the clients with whom I have enjoyed forming relationships, and the like-minded practitioners and thought leaders who share my commitment to transforming the world of innovation provide a continual source of inspiration. Special thanks to Chip Bergh, Patrick Blair, Bruce Brown, Ken Dobler, Brad Gambill, George Glackin, David Goulait, Vijay Govindarajan, Melanie Healey, Maurizio Marchesini, Rita McGrath, Keyne Monson, Bernard Nee, J. P. Orbeta, Teo Ming Kian, Peter Sims, Dave Ulmer, Colin Watts, Francis Yeoh, and Christoph Zrenner.

I am deeply appreciative of my long-term mentors—Clayton Christensen, Clark Gilbert, and Richard Foster—each of whom teaches me something new in every conversation.

Last, but certainly not least, thanks to my family. My parents, siblings, and in-laws make me feel like I'm around the corner from home, even though I now live thousands of miles away. Special thanks to my brother Michael—you know why. And, of course, to my immediate family. Charlie, your boundless enthusiasm is a perpetual source of inspiration. Holly, you melt my heart on a daily basis. Harry, we were so happy to welcome you to the world in this year. And Joanne: Every time I leave you it breaks my heart; every time we talk when I am on the road it lifts me up; every time I step off a plane back home I feel re-energized. To our next adventure.

—Scott D. Anthony
Seat 14F, Singapore Airline Flight 820
July 2011

ABOUT THE AUTHOR

SCOTT D. ANTHONY is Managing Director of Innosight Asia-Pacific. Based in Innosight's Singapore office, he leads its Asian operations and venture-capital investing activities (Innosight Ventures) and launched Innosight's business prototyping and piloting practice (Innosight Labs).

Scott's previous books are *Seeing What's Next: Using the Theories of Innovation to Predict Industry Change*; *The Innovator's Guide to Growth: Putting Disruptive Innovation to Work*; and *The Silver Lining: An Innovation Playbook for Uncertain Times*. He has written articles for publications such as the *Wall Street Journal*, *Harvard Business Review*, *Bloomberg BusinessWeek*, *Forbes*, *Sloan Management Review*, *Advertising Age*, *Marketing Management*, and *Chief Executive*. He has a regular column at Harvard Business Online (www.hbr.org).

Scott received a BA in economics, summa cum laude, from Dartmouth College and an MBA with high distinction from Harvard Business School, where he was a Baker Scholar. He lives in Singapore with his wife Joanne, sons Charlie and Harry, and daughter Holly.